W0080225

# EdgeAI for Algorithmic Government

Rajan Gupta · Sanjana Das · Saibal Kumar Pal

# EdgeAI
# for Algorithmic
# Government

Rajan Gupta
Research & Analytics Division
Analyttica Datalab
Bangalore, India

Sanjana Das
Deen Dayal Upadhyaya College
University of Delhi
Delhi, India

Saibal Kumar Pal
SAG Lab
Delhi, India

ISBN 978-981-19-9797-6          ISBN 978-981-19-9798-3   (eBook)
https://doi.org/10.1007/978-981-19-9798-3

© The Author(s), under exclusive license to Springer Nature Singapore Pte Ltd. 2023
This work is subject to copyright. All rights are solely and exclusively licensed by the Publisher, whether the whole or part of the material is concerned, specifically the rights of translation, reprinting, reuse of illustrations, recitation, broadcasting, reproduction on microfilms or in any other physical way, and transmission or information storage and retrieval, electronic adaptation, computer software, or by similar or dissimilar methodology now known or hereafter developed.
The use of general descriptive names, registered names, trademarks, service marks, etc. in this publication does not imply, even in the absence of a specific statement, that such names are exempt from the relevant protective laws and regulations and therefore free for general use.
The publisher, the authors, and the editors are safe to assume that the advice and information in this book are believed to be true and accurate at the date of publication. Neither the publisher nor the authors or the editors give a warranty, expressed or implied, with respect to the material contained herein or for any errors or omissions that may have been made. The publisher remains neutral with regard to jurisdictional claims in published maps and institutional affiliations.

Cover illustration: © Melisa Hasan

This Palgrave Macmillan imprint is published by the registered company Springer Nature Singapore Pte Ltd.
The registered company address is: 152 Beach Road, #21-01/04 Gateway East, Singapore 189721, Singapore

*Dedicated to*

My *"Gurumaa"* for holding my hand in Life,
My *"Parents"* for making me stand in Life,
My *"Nephews – Reyaansh & Atharva"* for making me strong in Life,
My *"Brother & His Wife"* for helping me progress in Life, and
My *"Wife"* for supporting and loving me unconditionally in Life!

—Dr. Rajan Gupta

My *"Family"* for always believing in me and supporting me.

—Sanjana Das

The memory of my *"Parents"*...

—Dr. Saibal Kumar Pal

# PREFACE

This book titled *EdgeAI for Algorithmic Government* has got three significant things to offer—Introduction to Algorithmic Government and Large-Scale Decision-Making, various computing technologies around Algorithmic Government like Cloud, Fog, Edge, and EdgeAI, followed by potential use cases of EdgeAI for Algorithmic Government around the world.

Algorithmic Government or Government by Algorithm is an emerging concept introduced around the world in recent years. It involves using Data Science and Artificial Intelligence for decision-making by the Government for various services and processes. Algorithms facilitating large-scale government decision-making processes and public services must be well structured, secure, and fast, resulting in transparent and righteous governance. The cloud-centric architecture of AI is no longer suitable for the rapid calculations and analysis that must be performed on such a massive volume of data. To this end, we need to bring the AI services closer to the user devices, i.e., at the edge of the network. This complimentary relationship of Edge Computing and AI is what we call EdgeAI or Edge Intelligence, which aims to realize the potential benefits of AI at the network edge instead of the network core.

The first chapter covers the background of Algorithmic Government, various concepts, motivations, and benefits, large-scale decision-making for government, and different technological solutions. The second chapter introduces the concept of Edge Computing and various types of

AI techniques used for analysis purposes for computing different tasks. The third chapter focuses on EdgeAI principles, levels of Edge Intelligence, and model training/inferencing at Edge. The fourth chapter presents various Algorithmic Government use cases where EdgeAI would be applicable and beneficial. Chapter five presents a combined framework for EdgeAI applications, network integrations, resource management, coexistence of cloud and edge, reliability of Edge devices, hardware level requirements, and future scope of work.

This book will serve as introductory material for the readers from technology, public policy, and management fields. It will help develop understanding around different concepts present for automated large-scale decision-making and usage of EdgeAI technology in the public sector as an advancement. The reader should differentiate E-Governance as the digitization of the Government processes, and Algorithmic Governance as the automated decision-making on behalf of the Government.

Bangalore, India                                        Rajan Gupta
Delhi, India                                            Sanjana Das
Delhi, India                                         Saibal Kumar Pal

# Acknowledgements

The authors of this book would like to gratefully and sincerely thank all the people who have supported them during the journey of writing this book, to only some of whom it is possible to mention here.

Primarily, the authors (Dr. Gupta and Dr. Pal) would like to thank their Ph.D. Supervisor—Prof. Sunil Kumar Muttoo, for his valuable guidance and research directions in the field of Computer Science and Data Science. Then the authors would like to thank current and former faculty members of the Department of Computer Science, University of Delhi—Prof. Vasudha Bhatnagar, Prof. Punam Bedi, Prof. Naveen Kumar, Prof. Neelima Gupta, Mr. P. K. Hazra, and Ms. Vidya Kulkarni. Also, the author (Dr. Gupta) would like to thank faculty members from Center of Information Technologies and Applied Mathematics, University of Nova Gorica, Slovenia, led by Prof. Tanja Urbancic, Prof. Irina, Prof. Nada, and Ms. Tea for their valuable support. And a special mention to Prof. Devendra Potnis from UTK, USA for his extremely helpful suggestions around developing research areas around Algorithmic Government. They all helped provide infrastructure and resources related to Doctoral and Post-doctoral Research work, which was in Data Science and E-Governance. The doctoral as well post-doctoral work became the basis for this book.

The author (Dr. Gupta) would also like to thank all the members of Analyttica Datalab, especially Research & Analytics Division. This book would not have been possible without the valuable support from members of Analyttica Family—Mr. Rajeev Baphna (CEO), Mr. Satyamoy Chatterjee (EVP), Mr. Chaitanya Pathak (CTO), Mr. Madhav Kaushik (SVP), and Mr. Koushal Udupa (CFO). The author (Ms. Das) would also like to thank the Administrative and Teaching Unit of Deen Dayal Upadhyaya College, University of Delhi, under the guidance of Dr. Hemchand Jain, for providing their support toward the writing of this book. The author (Dr. Pal) would like to thank the Defense Research and Development Organization (DRDO) authorities, Government of India, for providing valuable inputs toward the research work carried out for this book.

Finally, this work would not have been possible without the invaluable support from the publishing team of Palgrave Macmillan, Springer, esp. Ms. Sandeep Kaur, Ms. Aishwarya Balachandar, and Ms. Sagarika Ghosh. This book also recognizes incredible support from the book's endorsers, and the authors' guru, mentors, family, and friends. So the authors would like to thank them all from the bottom of their hearts.

# CONTENTS

# ABOUT THE AUTHORS

**Dr. Rajan Gupta** is a Research and Analytics Professional with 13+ years of combined experience in Research, Analytical Consulting, Training, and Teaching in the field of Data Science. He has authored one patent, four books, and more than seventy-five research papers in the area of Public Information Systems, E-Governance, Algorithmic Government, Data Science, Technology, and Management. He has received prestigious "AI Changemaker Leader Award" under 3AI ACME Awards at BEYOND 2023 and "40 Under 40 Data Scientists" award for 2022 by Analytics India Magazine at MLDS 2022.

He is currently heading Research & Analytics (R&A) Division of Analyttica Datalab Inc (as Vice President—Research & Analytics), which is a contextual Data Science and Machine Learning platform company in experiental AI/ML and Analytics EdTech space at global level. He is responsible for converting client request into skilling path for working professionals through unique methodology of "Learn, Apply and Solve" available through ATH LEAPS platform. The R&A division is the "Think Tank" of Analyttica, driven by customer delight, client requirements, market needs, and innovation, managing the following aspects of the firm:

- Develop analytics-oriented course structure for quick learning of concepts by professionals across various industries and domains.

- Implement analytical algorithms on platform for helping business leaders and managers to work on point-n-click functionality for function execution.
- Identification of business problems and relevant datasets for simulating real-time work environment for the learners.
- Create user experience through applied content and use cases.
- Deliver knowledge sessions, hands-on workshops, and technical talks for upskilling of data science professionals.
- Innovate through intellectual property development by filing patents, writing research papers, white papers, reports, and business cases.

He has done his Ph.D. in Information Systems and Analytics from the Department of Computer Science, University of Delhi and Postdoc in Data Science and Data Modelling from Center of Information Technologies and Applied Mathematics, University of Nova Gorica, Slovenia, Europe. He is triple post-graduate and completed his Master in Computer Application (MCA) from the University of Delhi; Post Graduate Program in Management (PGPM) from IMT Ghaziabad (CDL); and Executive Program in Business Intelligence and Analytics (EPBABI) from IIM-Ranchi. He is UGC NET-JRF qualified and holds a certificate in Consulting from Consultancy Development Centre (CDC), DSIR, Ministry of Science and Technology, Government of India. He is one of the few Certified Analytics Professional (CAP-INFORMS) around the world and is serving as CAP Ambassador in Asia Region. He is the first non-US member of the prestigious Analytics Certification Board (ACB) of INFORMS, USA. He has also been accredited with 'Graduate Statistician' from the American Statistical Association (ASA).

He has worked on various analytical consulting assignments at national and international level on problems related to the areas of Digital Government, Healthcare, Education, Retail, and Insurance. He has delivered lectures at the University of Delhi, KIIT University, and IMT—Ghaziabad in Computer Science, Data Science, Information Security, and Management. He has also conducted several 1:1 live mentoring and training sessions related to upskilling of analytical career, preparations for analytical certifications, and technical knowledge on Analytics Project Lifecycle for various data science professionals from reputed organizations like Verizon, Nokia, Cyient, Tech Mahindra, TCS, Ericsson, and Anthem.

His area of interest includes Data Science, E-Governance, Algorithmic Government, Public Information Systems, and Information Security. He has contributed to the E-Governance Development Index report by the United Nations (EGDI-2020). He is a member of the reviewer panel of multiple international journals and conferences including prestigious ICEGOV. He has also delivered a talk as a panelist on Data Science Application for E-Governance on an international forum sponsored by International Data Engineering and Science Association (IDEAS), USA, and conducted a Global Workshop on "Inclusion of Marginalized Communities" through Electronic Governance and Analytics at ICEGOV-2020 hosted by United Nations University.

LinkedIn Profile: https://www.linkedin.com/in/rajan-gupta-cap/.

**Ms. Sanjana Das** is pursuing her Bachelor's degree in Computer Science from Deen Dayal Upadhaya College, University of Delhi. Her fields of interest include Artificial Intelligence, Cloud Computing, Edge Computing, and EdgeAI. This book is Sanjana's first research project, and along with gaining knowledge about avant-garde technologies in Computer Science, she has also learned the skills of patience and resilience. She is highly enthusiastic about research work and plans to pursue a doctorate from a global university.

**Dr. Saibal Kumar Pal** is a Senior Scientist with Scientific Analysis Group (SAG) Lab, Defense Research and Development Organization, Government of India, for many years and has been awarded "Scientist of the Year" from the Government of India. He received his Ph.D. in Computer Science from the University of Delhi and is an Invited Faculty and Research Guide at several national institutions. His areas of interest are Information and Network Security, Computational Intelligence, Information Systems, and Electronic Governance. He has more than 250 publications in books, journals, and international conference proceedings. He has contributed to a number of significant projects and international collaborations and is a member of national advisory committees.

# Abbreviations

| | |
|---|---|
| AI | Artificial Intelligence |
| ANN | Artificial Neural Network |
| ARDV | Autonomous Rural Delivery Vehicle |
| CBP | US Customs and Border Protection |
| CCPA | California Consumer Privacy Act |
| CFPB | Consumer Financial Protection Bureau, USA |
| CIM | Compute-In-Memory |
| CIRA | Corporate Issuer Risk Assessment |
| CNN | Convolution Neural Networks |
| CPU | Central Processing Unit |
| CRP | Consensus Reaching Processes |
| CV | Computer Vision |
| DBSCAN | Density-Based Spatial Clustering of Applications with Noise |
| DDS | Disability Determination Service, USA |
| DL | Deep Learning |
| DMs | Decision-Makers |
| DNN | Deep Neural Network |
| EdgeAI | Edge Artificial Intelligence |
| EI | Edge Intelligence |
| ETSI | European Telecommunications Standards Institute |
| FedAvg | Federated Averaging |
| FL | Federated Learning |
| GDPR | General Data Protection Regulation |
| GMM | Gaussian Mixture Models |
| GoSGD | Gossip Stochastic Gradient Descent |
| GPU | Graphical Processing Unit |

| | |
|---|---|
| GTDP | Greedy Two-Dimensional Partition |
| IoT | Internet of Things |
| KPIs | Key Performance Indicators |
| LDA | Latent Dirichlet Allocation |
| LSDM | Large-Scale Decision-Making |
| MCDM | Multi-Criteria Decision-Making |
| MEC | Mobile Edge Computing |
| ML | Machine Learning |
| NLP | Natural Language Processing |
| Non-IIID | Non-Independent Identical Distribution |
| PE | Processing Elements |
| PII | Personally Identifiable Information |
| QDD | Quick Disability Determination |
| RMSE | Root Mean Squared Error |
| RNN | Recurrent Neural Networks |
| RRAM | Resistive Random-Access Memory |
| SEC | Security and Exchange Commissions, USA |
| SGD | Stochastic Gradient Descent |
| SIRFC | Sparse Representation-based Intuitionistic Fuzzy Clustering |
| SMCD | Structured Model Compact Deployment |
| SNA | Social Network Analysis |
| SSA | Social Security Administration, USA |
| STM | Structured Topic Model |
| SURTRAC | Scalable Urban Traffic Control |
| USPS | United States Postal Service |
| VM | Virtual Machines |

# LIST OF FIGURES

# LIST OF TABLES

# CHAPTER 1

# Algorithmic Government

**Abstract** In this chapter, we introduce the concept of Algorithmic Government and highlight the motivations and benefits of AI in governance by reviewing several use cases. We then discuss the importance of Large-Scale Decision-Making (LSDM) events in the context of Algorithmic Government and talk about relevant definitions, characteristics of LSDM events, and the different consensus reaching processes. We also elaborate on the various ways AI is integrated into LSDM events to enhance its efficacy. Next, we discuss the shortcomings of the cloud and fog architectures currently used to implement AI in federal agencies. The issues identified are latency, communication overhead, and bandwidth consumption, focusing on security and privacy concerns. Finally, we discuss these challenges and drive demand for new computing technologies.

**Keywords** Algorithmic Government · Public services · Artificial Intelligence · Large-Scale Decision-Making · Cloud computing · Fog computing

© The Author(s), under exclusive license to Springer Nature
Singapore Pte Ltd. 2023
R. Gupta et al., *EdgeAI for Algorithmic Government*,
https://doi.org/10.1007/978-981-19-9798-3_1

## 1.1    Background

Government automation achieved through predictive behavior analysis of Artificial Intelligence (AI), Block chain, and Big Data is destined to change the government's infrastructure, decision-making processes, and overall operation. AI has been used to deliver public services in smart cities, smart healthcare, smart education, and smart municipal services. Municipal services include smart energy meters in every house, real-time monitoring of traffic, adaptable street lighting, smart waste and water management, and more. Moreover, intelligent services are not only aimed at helping citizens but also government officials. Robo-advisors (To assist the civil officers), smart contracts, and data management through block chain ledgers are some common applications revolutionizing government agencies (Engin & Treleaven, 2019). The advances in Machine Learning (ML) and data collection have automated previously impossible processes. However, if not controlled carefully, the dark side of AI can overshadow the positive benefits of technology. Hence, the design and implementation of the Algorithmic Governance system must ensure its effectiveness and legitimacy (Danaher et al., 2017).

## 1.2    Motivation and Benefits

Designing and implementing algorithms the right way can enable government services to reallocate resources more effectively and ultimately serve citizens with unprecedented efficiency. Besides the known benefits of AI including faster and more accurate decision-making, 24 × 7 availability, reduced human error, and repetitive task performance, the integration of algorithms into government services enjoys many more benefits which we have illustrated by reviewing the use cases compiled by Engstrom et al. (2020). Figure 1.1 gives an overview of the benefits of AI in governance.

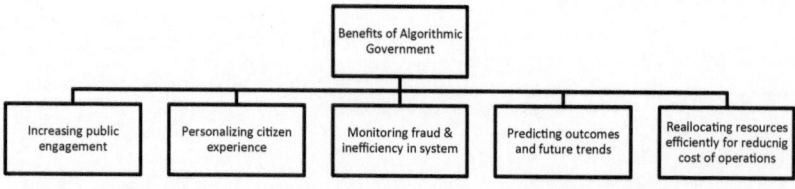

**Fig. 1.1**   Benefits of Algorithmic Government for citizens and administrators

**Public Engagement and Personalizing Citizen Experience**: AI is being incorporated in administrative agencies to simplify and improve the quality of government-citizen interactions. Customer services like filling out official forms (license, passport, etc.) and answering citizens' questions are being initiated through chatbots and open data portals. The Consumer Financial Protection Bureau (CFPB, USA) utilizes Natural Language Processing (NLP) to process consumer complaints. NLP helps in assisting CFPB's limited resource capacity to analyze and categorize thousands of complaints submitted weekly. The primary use of NLP includes removing Personally Identifiable Information (PII) from the Consumer Complaint Database and organizing the complaints through topic modeling. The former takes place in three steps, involving an open-source computer software to identify nouns and verbs, thereby initiating the scrubbing process of PII, followed by verification of the effectiveness of the automated scrubbing process by a trained human reviewer and a quality assurance specialist. The topic modeling process includes classifying the comments submitted via a Structured Topic Model (STM) that leverages Latent Dirichlet Allocation (LDA). CFPB publicly shares the complaints in the Consumer Complaint Database after removing the PII and categorizing the complaints. As a result, companies are allowed to acknowledge publicly and provide resolutions for the complaints submitted by the consumers.

**Monitoring fraud, inefficiency, and inaccuracy in public services**: The Security and Exchange Commissions (SEC, USA) has devised the Corporate Issuer Risk Assessment (CIRA) to maintain a fair and efficient market. The financial reports of corporate issuers can be 100 pages long, consisting of complex information like financial data, risk factors, business information, and the likes. Processing and analyzing these reports require a lot of resources. CIRA leverages 200 metrics to detect anomalies and identify the corporate filers who need further investigation, thereby effectively utilizing the existing limited resources. Misconduct or possible fraud is detected using a random forest model trained on a historical dataset of past issuer filings considering indicators such as past enforcement actions and earnings restatements. SEC personnel review the model results, taking into consideration some other metrics, thus improving the regulatory analysis of capital and labor market.

**Predicting outcomes and future trends**: The Social Security Administration (SSA) essentially determines whether a claimant is entitled to disability benefits or not. The implementation to determine whether an applicant meets the criteria involves a rigorous five-step process. SSA leverages an AI model to predict the claimants with the most likelihood of qualifying for benefits at the initial application filing phase to accelerate this process. After each referral, as indicated by the model, the state Disability Determination Service (DDS) appoints a Quick Disability Determination (QDD) unit, wherein an examiner and a medical expert sign-off the claim. The AI model is even used at the hearing level to predict which claims are likely to receive benefits after being denied reconsideration. The claims with a higher chance of success are moved earlier in the queue than cases with a lower predicted probability of receiving benefits. Hence, using prediction algorithms trained on past medical findings, records, and treatment protocols, AI has helped improve and speed up the case processes tremendously.

**Reallocating resources efficiently for reducing cost of operation**: The United States Postal Service (USPS) handles about half of the world's mail volume, and hence its effectiveness is crucial. Recently, the personnel cost (76% of the Postal Service expenses) has increased due to increasing labor-intensive deliveries. The cost of accidents and rising fuel costs also need to be considered. Autonomous vehicles and Long-haul trucks have been introduced to tackle the aforementioned challenges. Computer AI uses data captured from human drivers in response to audio-visual road cues to train the model on driving techniques. The data collected from the sensors are combined with detailed digital maps that show road layout, speed limits, and other navigation-related information. The University of Michigan devised the Autonomous Rural Delivery Vehicle (ARDV) protocol to conduct the autonomous delivery process on less congested rural routes. A human postal carrier was present, sorting the mail between stops and delivering the packages out of the window. The agency partnered with TuSimple, an independent long-haul truck company, for testing their second AI application. USPS trailers were hauled between Phoenix, Arizona, Dallas, and Texas during the two-week pilot program. The pilot program was not completely autonomous like the ARDV, but yielded excellent results in terms of speed of package deliveries and no accidents whatsoever. As the personnel required are considerably less and the fuel costs are saved due to faster delivery trips, the operation price has reduced dramatically.

## 1.3  Large-Scale Decision-Making

Government agencies and civil servants make countless decisions every day. The impact of these decisions on people's lives can be life-changing. No decision-making process is infallible, but the government has the responsibility to provide transparency, accountability, and attractiveness commensurate with the impact of decision-making. Moreover, with the increase of citizens' awareness of democracy and the overflow of data from various sources, Large-Scale Decision-Making (LSDM) is gaining a lot of popularity (Tang & Liao, 2021). LSDM events are different from small group ones as the decisions made during this event generally impact society or a significant number of people. Numerous diverse stakeholders consider multiple criteria for assessing the alternatives. LSDM focuses on reaching a high consensus among participants, crucial for government decision-making scenarios. A unanimous agreement with minimum conflict will result in better public services. To do justice to the opinions and interests of most citizens, AI integrates publicly available information into decision-making processes. For example, when the United States Postal Services proposed the autonomous postal vehicles, opinions from the citizens were taken via an online survey regarding their thoughts on autonomous delivery (Engstrom et al., 2020). Using AI technologies like opinion mining and sentiment analysis, public opinion can be considered, leading to a better government-citizen relationship. In this section, we will review the characteristics of a Large-Scale Decision-Making event, the phases of consensus reaching processes and the implementation of AI in LSDM.

LSDM events are different than other decision-making events, as the alternatives are assessed under multiple criteria, and the entire decision process is very complex and dynamic. If a limited set of alternatives are evaluated under multiple criteria, with no less than 20 stakeholders participating in a dynamic decision-making process aimed at reducing the conflict among Decision-Makers (DMs) or maximizing the support for the final decision, then the decision-making event is referred to as a Large-Scale Decision-Making event. LSDM events can be summarized by the following characteristics:

a. In an LSDM event, alternatives are assessed under multiple criteria, presenting a higher complexity than other group decision-making events. It is a particular class of Multi-Criteria Decision-Making (MCDM) events.

b. Multiple stakeholders/decision-makers are involved in an LSDM event. The size of the group will be considerable if the DMs participating include all the communities of the affected stakeholders. Therefore, no less than 20 DMs should be present for the event to be considered as an LSDM event.

c. LSDM events are complex and dynamic as they aim at achieving either or both of the two things: (i) maximizing the support among DMs for the final decision (ii) reducing as much disagreement as possible, among DMs.

**Consensus Reaching Processes (CRP)**: Large decision events typically involve a variety of DMs with different interests and preferences, representing stakeholders from diverse backgrounds. Therefore, if no dynamic feedback mechanism is used and decisions are made based solely on initial evaluation information, it is likely that some DMs will not be satisfied with this decision. This can harm the affected community. Therefore, if the consensus threshold is not reached in the initial evaluation of alternatives, CRP proceeds by applying some or all of the following phases, as has been summarized by Ding et al. (2020).

**Clustering Phase**: The Decision-Makers are divided into groups based on their similarites, relationships, or deviation from the collective opinion. Members in the same cluster are considered to exhibit similar performance. For example, if a group is identified as the least cooperative, then preference modification feedbacks are provided to all members of that cluster. The clustering process is also dynamic, and the clusters can change with each iteration. In Sparse Representation-based Intuitionistic Fuzzy Clustering (SIRFC), the clusters are formed based on the relationships of the DMs. The two primary algorithms of SRIFC are SIRFC-E (The cluster with the strongest relationships) and SIRFC-S (The clusters with a soft relationship strength). The relationships among DMs in these clusters can be used to identify the key figures and leaders.

**Non-Cooperative Detection Phase**: Few stakeholders may be obdurate about keeping their initial evaluations unchanged. They can have a negative impact on CRPs and hence they must be identified. Most non-cooperative detection approaches leverage the distance of individual DMs or clusters from the collective opinion. Other approaches consider the extent of cooperativeness. The DMs with a degree less than a preset threshold are categorized as non-cooperative decision-makers. The weights of assessments done by these non-cooperative decision-makers are usually penalized, and the weights of cooperative DMs are positively updated.

**Weight Penalization Phase**: Initialization of weights at the beginning of an LSDM is not compulsory. However, if the DMs are experts in their fields, then the organizer of the LSDM event can assign weights to the DM distinguishing their professional levels. Preference modifications are first suggested to the DMs or clusters having the farthest distance from the collective opinion. DMs who adjust according to the suggestions made are classified as cooperative, and the DMs that ignore or oppose the suggestions are considered non-cooperative. Accordingly, the weights are penalized or updated commensurate with the DMs cooperativeness. The product of a DMs' weight multiplied with his/her assessment is considered in the final selection of the alternatives. Hence, the updated weights of cooperative DMs can reduce the negative impact of the assessments made by non-cooperative DMs. Furthermore, the weight updating rules can be incentivized by declaring them at the beginning of the LSDM event, thus promoting cooperative behavior among DMs.

**Feedback and Preference Modification Phase**: The DMs who contribute less to the CRPs are requested to modify their assessment. The more precise the detection of the DMs is, the easier it will be to accept the suggestion, which will improve the CRP efficiency to a great extent. Assessing the DMs' behaviors parallelly with the decision-making processes helps to identify attributes of DMs other than their cooperativeness (such as reliability, overconfidence behavior). This, in turn, can help provide better suggestions of modifications personalized to the DMs. Usually, the amendments suggested aim at minimizing the distance between the DMs' and the collective opinion. Some approaches leverage optimization models to decrease the conflict degree or increase the consensus degree as much as possible. The calculated modified assessments can be provided as recommendations to the DMs. Their weights are either penalized or updated depending on their willingness to act on the recommendations.

## 1.4    Implementation of AI in LSDM

Decision-making processes in algorithmic government are increasingly depending on AI and Big Data, due to the presence of a plethora of data sources, which are seen as a beneficial resource for the DMs to help make informed decisions. To handle such humongous volume of data, artificial intelligence is needed. For example, in policy-making decisions, the public's input could be valuable and extracted from publicly available information on the Internet. Furthermore, data fusion technologies can also help form better groups in the clusters process, utilizing a DMs' behavior pattern during previous LSDM events, their social background, preferences, interests, and the likes.

**Machine Learning Methods**: Clustering models are used in the aforementioned clustering phase of a CRP to help divide large groups into manageable smaller groups. Data points are grouped based on their similarity using clustering models such as K-means and Density-based spatial clustering of applications with noise (DBSCAN) among others. Clustering can help reduce the complexity of LSDM, detect non-cooperative behavior easily, and identify common opinion patterns and key figures and leaders in a subgroup. Anomaly detection is also used to identify assessments (data points) that deviate significantly from other opinions (rest of the data).

**Computational Neuroscience**: The fusion of neuroscience and AI could be very valuable in the context of LSDM events. The neural process behind the interactions of DMs and the dilemma between one's own preference vs the group's preference can be utilized to make CRPs more efficient. This can also help decipher the reasons for non-cooperative behavior in some DMs.

**Deep Learning methods**: Deep Learning has become the cynosure of AI in recent years. It can be especially utilized when multiple criteria are interrelated. Deep learning can help measure parameters of a decision-making model, the parameter settings for aggregation operator, and weights of DMs based on their past behavior in LSDM events, social interactions, interests, and the likes.

**Autonomous Intelligent Agents**: Research shows that autonomous agents can exhibit the cognitive abilities required for decision-making and work individually and collectively. In the coming years, hybrid LSDM can become a reality where artificial participants representing affected communities will work along with human DMs. The rationality of human DMs has been combined with AI's fast data processing skills in an Environmental Crisis Management system. Autonomous agents can also aid in policy-making, urban planning, e-governance, etc., using Social Media Analysis Natural Language Processing and to analyze the sentiments of the affected communities, thus automatically creating a preference structure.

**Group Recommender Systems**: AI algorithm-based decision support tools provide users with personalized services and products commensurate with their interests and preferences. Simple fusion technologies are used in tourism or entertainment industries to combine individual preferences into a group (collective) preference or consolidate personal lists of preference items into recommended items for a group. The fusion of recommender systems and LSDM can promote to consentient recommendations for all members in the same cluster. In tourism situations subdividing a larger group into sub-groups can help maximize personal travel satisfaction. Recommender Systems can assist in decision-making for large groups, for example, providing recommendations of restaurants for business teams or consensual music for people in a fitness club.

## 1.5   COMPUTING ISSUES WITH ALGORITHMIC GOVERNMENT

The AI technologies and algorithms implemented in public services, law enforcement, decision-making, etc., are usually deployed in a cloud or fog environment. Both computing technologies have gained a lot of popularity over the years due to their on-demand access to data storage locations, network administration, servers, and cost-effectiveness. However, data transmission from the end devices or fog nodes to the central cloud poses challenges of latency, privacy, and consumption of enormous resources. To make an algorithmic government well-founded, efficient, and coherent, the base of operation of the AI services, i.e., the computing technologies have to be reliable. Therefore, we must first identify the challenges of cloud computing and fog computing to understand the need for new computing technology better.

Security is one of the most important and daunting concern in cloud and fog computing. The storage, analysis, and processing of user data at another location on a different hard disk raises several user privacy threats. Shared resources on the same physical machine invite unwanted secondary channels between malevolent and genuine resources. Large-scale decision-making processes in the government or public services like filling up important forms may require privacy sensitive data from the public. Malicious insiders to the cloud provider can get hold of this user data and steal personal information such as medical records, financial records, social security numbers, passwords, passport numbers, and much more. The data from Smart grids or Smart meters can also be used to analyze an end user's habits, such as the programs he/she prefers to watch or even when the user is not at home. Data breaches, phishing, and account hijacking are many risks that users and organizations are exposed to.

In the context of fog computing specifically, many privacy and security issues need to be taken care of, summarized by Mukherjee et al. (2017). The fog network involves the interplay of various devices, and hence each of them needs to exhibit trust in one another. Moreover, the trust between the fog nodes and Internet of Things (IoT) devices is also required. The IoT devices which send their data to the fog nodes should validate whether the fog devices are safe or not. Likewise, the fog nodes receiving the processing requests from the IoT devices should verify if the devices are harmful or ingenuine. Authentication of devices connected to the fog network is also required. Still, the traditional authentication methods such as certificates and Public-Key Infrastructures are not compatible with the resource-constrained user devices. A Denial-of-Service attack becomes very easy to launch since most of the devices in the fog network are not mutually authenticated. This attack occurs in the form of a compromised node making infinite requests for storage or processing facilities. When several malfunctioning nodes make repeated requests simultaneously, the graveness of the attack intensifies, hampering the path of genuine requests made from legitimate IoT devices. Moreover, the fog nodes in the vicinity of IoT devices may receive privacy-sensitive information from the devices, which may expose the user's personal information to a malicious attacker.

Besides the security and privacy issues in cloud and fog, the challenges of latency, communication overhead, and bandwidth consumption are also persistent. Especially in hybrid clouds, the overhead communication increases significantly as a user or organization's data is spread across various private or public clouds. In situations where a user has split data among multiple clouds (For example, to protect confidential data), the cost of integrating data can be considerable as different clouds have different interfaces and patented protocols. Even though reducing latency is one of the main benefits of fog, in pressing situations such as healthcare services or time-constrained decision-making processes, even faster processing and response time are required. For example, a fog service has been proposed by Ali et al. to detect heart attacks through smartwatches leveraging motion control and voice control. This service is proposed to improve the real-time response time to these detected distress calls. However, even a few seconds of delay in detecting the heart attack or processing the request can lead to a life-or-death situation. Hence, we need to bring the computing services even closer to the users to make algorithmic government more efficient. Therefore, we introduce the concept of edge computing for Algorithmic Government, as covered in the subsequent chapters.

## 1.6    Summary

In this chapter, we first introduce the concept of Algorithmic Government by illustrating some already existing examples of AI being integrated into various sectors of the government. We then focused on the motivation of algorithms in the government (increasing public engagement and personalizing citizen experience, monitoring fraud, inefficiency, and inaccuracy in public services, predicting outcomes and future trends, reallocating resources efficiently for reducing cost of operation) by reviewing various use cases of artificial intelligence in government agencies (Engstrom et al., 2020). This is followed by an introduction to Large-Scale Decision-Making events and how they fit into government run by algorithms. We then provided a proper definition of LSDM events, a brief introduction to consensus reaching processes and its various phases, and the implementation of AI in LSDM events. We then discuss the computing issues in algorithmic government, i.e., the disadvantages of the currently used cloud and fog architecture for the implementation of AI in federal agencies. The problems highlighted are that of latency, communication overhead, and bandwidth consumption with a particular focus on security and privacy concerns. Finally, we discuss these challenges to provide a motivation for the need of a new computing technology, i.e., Edge computing.

# REFERENCES

Danaher, J., Hogan, M. J., Noone, C., Kennedy, R., Behan, A., De Paor, A., Felzmann, H., Haklay, M., Khoo, S.-M., Morison, J., Murphy, M. H., O'Brolchain, N., Schafer, B., & Shankar, K. (2017). Algorithmic governance: Developing a research agenda through the power of collective intelligence. *Big Data & Society, 4*(2), 2053951717726554.

Ding, R. X., Palomares, I., Wang, X., Yang, G. R., Liu, B., Dong, Y., Herrera-Viedma, E., & Herrera, F. (2020). Large-scale decision-making: Characterization, taxonomy, challenges and future directions from an Artificial Intelligence and applications perspective. *Information Fusion, 59*, 84–102.

Engin, Z., & Treleaven, P. (2019). Algorithmic government: Automating public services and supporting civil servants in using data science technologies. *The Computer Journal, 62*(3), 448–460.

Engstrom, D. F., Ho, D. E., Sharkey, C. M., & Cuéllar, M. F. (2020). *Government by algorithm: Artificial intelligence in federal administrative agencies* (NYU School of Law, Public Law Research Paper [20–54]).

Mukherjee, M., Matam, R., Shu, L., Maglaras, L., Ferrag, M. A., Choudhury, N., & Kumar, V. (2017). Security and privacy in fog computing: Challenges. *IEEE Access, 5*, 19293–19304.

Tang, M., & Liao, H. (2021). From conventional group decision making to large-scale group decision making: What are the challenges and how to meet them in big data era? A state-of-the-art survey. *Omega, 100*, 102141.

# CHAPTER 2

# Edge Computing

**Abstract** This chapter focuses on discussing the two key components of EdgeAI, i.e., Edge Computing and Artificial Intelligence. We first explain the concept of Edge Computing, and talk about few related or commonly confused terms to encourage a better understanding of the Edge paradigm in isolation. Next, we review certain applications of Edge Computing, thereby highlight its motivation and benefits. We then provide a comparative analysis of cloud, fog, and edge architectures, discussing the various aspects in which they differ. This is followed by discussion on the next component of EdgeAI, i.e., Artificial Intelligence. We provide brief overviews of commonly adopted AI models, with a special emphasis on Deep Neural Networks. We discuss the basic working of Artificial Neural Networks, finally building up to the more advanced Convolution Neural Networks and Recurrent Neural Networks.

**Keywords** Edge Computing · Artificial Intelligence · Cloud computing · Fog Computing · Regression models · Classification models · Deep Neural Networks · Convolution Neural Networks · Recurrent Neural Networks

© The Author(s), under exclusive license to Springer Nature Singapore Pte Ltd. 2023
R. Gupta et al., *EdgeAI for Algorithmic Government*,
https://doi.org/10.1007/978-981-19-9798-3_2

## 2.1    Emergence of Edge Computing

Edge Computing is a new computing paradigm which brings the storage and computational facilities of the cloud closer to the user. In edge computing, the data storage, processing, and analysis happens locally, i.e., on the end user's device itself. One of the most significant advantages of edge computing is its ability to reduce latency significantly, as data does not have to traverse to a cloud or data center. Real-time analysis of the data collected in an autonomous vehicle is essential since even milliseconds matter on a busy road. Edge is also highly versatile, i.e., it can perform operations with the same ease for a single user or for, let's say, a million users. Since smart operations are not dependent on a stable internet connection to the cloud, edge computing also improves reliability. The edge is therefore characterized by quick response time, deeper insights due to the opportunity of accessing more application data, comprehensive data analysis, and increased Quality of Experience. The advantages and benefits of edge computing hence seem very promising for revolutionizing the IoT industry.

**Some Related Terms**: A cloudlet as first proposed by Satyanarayanan et al. (2009), can be thought of as a "data center in a box" which brings the powerful computational resources of a cloud physically closer to mobile devices or IoT devices. It leverages low latency and high-bandwidth connectivity to provide cloud features such as Virtual Machines in physical proximity to limited bandwidth applications requiring near real-time response. The European Telecommunications Standards Institute (ETSI) introduced Mobile Edge Computing (MEC) which is a concept similar to cloudlet, but instead of a data center, the computational resources are utilized by mobile devices from a base station. Cisco coined the term Fog Computing, which is essentially an extension of the cloud computing paradigm, bringing storage and computational resources from the core of the network to the edge of the network. It facilitates the execution of applications in the edge of the network through smartly connected devices. Yi et al. (2015) provide a more general definition of Fog Computing—It is a computing architecture comprising one or more connected devices at the edge of the network necessarily supported by cloud services, which work in a collaborative manner to provide storage and computation resources to clients present in close proximity.

## 2.2   APPLICATION OF EDGE COMPUTING

With the rapid growth in IoT Devices and big data applications like smart homes, smart cities, smart healthcare, and smart education, the computing requirements are ever-increasing. Now more than ever, we need to bring the computations closer to the edge, i.e., the user devices. This section will review several case studies where edge computing performs better than cloud or fog computing. Even though all the case studies are not directly related to algorithmic government, they will highlight the capabilities and benefits of edge, making it a better computing paradigm than cloud or fog computing.

**Smart City**: Smart cities uses technology to improve the efficiency of government-provided services and improve the quality of life for its residents. A city of 1 million people will produce 180 million gigabytes of data per day through smart healthcare, smart municipal services, smart education, etc. Since edge computing is highly scalable and can be expanded from a single home to an entire city, it is perfect for operating a smart city. In the case of cloud computing, all this user data will be stored and processed in a central cloud, which is not viable as it will tremendously crowd the cloud servers. Applications requiring real-time low latency responses such as healthcare services or public safety services can no longer rely on the cloud. Edge can help make faster decisions by processing the data on the IoT device itself. Moreover, edge is context and location-aware; hence it is perfect for smart transportation management.

**E-Commerce**: About 2 billion people around the world buy their goods and services online. The reasonable prices, diverse variety of products, and speed delivery are more attractive than the hassles of shopping physically. In the case of shopping online, whenever a customer makes changes to his/her cart, the changes take place in the cloud and then are reflected on the user's cart. Figure 2.1 illustrates data and operations are cached to the edge nodes, which are then reverted to the user devices for e-commerce applications. This process might take a long time to execute due to the overflowing number of online customers and the relatively low network bandwidth of mobile phones. Since most of the online shopping is done from mobile phones, the shopping cart's updating process on the cloud is not preferred. Caching the data and operations performed on the cart (such as increasing the quantity of an item, adding or deleting an item, etc.) to the edge nodes can drastically reduce the latency. Modifications made to the shopping cart via the edge nodes are immediately reflected on the user's device.

**Multimedia Processing and Analytics**: Large volumes of images, videos, and audio are constantly being generated by IoT devices and mobile phones, which need to be analyzed quickly for some decision-making. Due to the bandwidth consumption, latency, and privacy issues of the cloud, it is no longer suitable for video analytics. For example, a speedy response time is essential if video analytics is used for a critical situation, such as spotting a criminal in a marketplace or an airport. Now, in a city or an airport, there are numerous cameras deployed for safety purposes, as well as there are mobile phones and other devices which may have captured the photo of that criminal. However, all images are not uploaded to a central cloud due to limited storage or security issues. Even if all the photos from every camera in that area were uploaded, it would take time to analyze them and spot the criminal. Hence, a central cloud can generate a request for searching that criminal, and all the edge devices can perform this request. If a device finds a relevant image on its local camera data, it reverts the result to the cloud. The use of edge computing can significantly reduce the time for such analytics and enhance the efficiency of many public services.

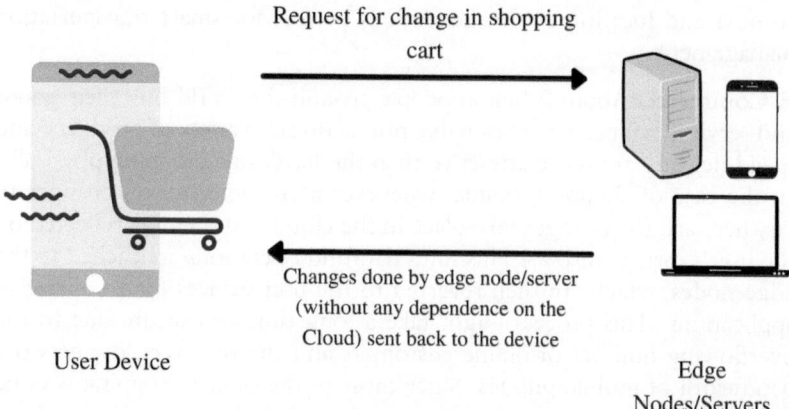

**Fig. 2.1** Data and operations are cached to the edge nodes, which are then reverted to the user devices for e-commerce applications

**Smart Fitness Devices**: Almost everyone today can be seen wearing a fitness watch or any other fitness capturing device, which calculates the heart rate, burnt calories, the number of steps walked, and even a person's oxygen levels. If the data from the watch is sent to the cloud, it can lead to unreliable connectivity between the watch sensor and the cloud and high communication latency. If an electrocardiogram (ECG) sensor is inbuilt in the watch, the edge device needs to take the decisions locally in case of critical events since time is of the essence. Figure 2.2 shows how the smart watch, edge server, and cloud server communicate with each other to make dynamic decisions. The working process starts with the wearable device sending its data to the smartphone. The smartphone app periodically checks the smartwatch to ensure that its connection is stable. Since the watch and the edge device are both resource-constrained, it is very likely that the smartphone may run out of storage. The data can be sent to the cloud or a fog node in such a case. However, the software must be developed in such a way that frequent transmissions of data to the cloud are avoided, and critical decisions take place on the device itself.

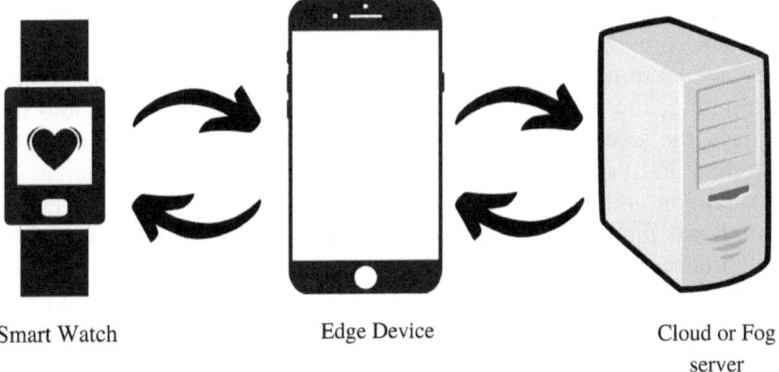

Smart Watch                        Edge Device                        Cloud or Fog
                                                                      server

**Fig. 2.2** Data generated by the smartwatch and the responsibility of decision-making to be taken on the data are constantly exchanged between the smartwatch, edge device, and the cloud or fog server

## 2.3    COMPARATIVE ANALYSIS
## OF CLOUD, FOG, AND EDGE COMPUTING

Cloud Computing is a computing paradigm that provides on-demand storage, analysis, networking, and intelligence without any direct management by a user. Cloud uses dynamic optimization to facilitate sharing of resources and generally utilizes a "pay-as-you-go" model. Depending on the requirements of a user or organization, they can opt for one of the three deployments of cloud service—public cloud, private cloud, hybrid cloud. The cloud offers Infrastructure as a service (IaaS), Platform as a Service (PaaS), Serverless computing and Software as a service (SaaS) to provide on-demand services like storage and networking, environment for developing and managing software applications, and delivering software applications over the Internet without having to worry about the underlying infrastructure. Edge computing is an advanced version of cloud furnishing storage, analysis and networking services closer to the user. Despite having a similar purpose, the edge and cloud paradigm differ in a number of respects. The main difference between the two is location of storage and compute resources. In Edge computing, these resources lie in the edge network, i.e., close to the data-producing devices, and in cloud computing, they are located within the Internet, which may or may not be in proximity to users. Compared to the low latency in edge computing, the greater the distance between the cloud servers and user devices, the greater the latency induced. Moreover, edge computing uses a decentralized architecture for the distribution of compute resources and the training and inference of AI models, whereas the cloud leverages a centralized model where all the resources exist in a single data center. The edge paradigm is characterized by location and context awareness and hence supports high mobility which are features not supported by the cloud. Laws to protect data privacy such as European Union's GDPR can cause legal issues in case the data has to be transmitted across regional and national boundaries in case of cloud computing. Local processing of data in edge computing not only evades privacy and legal issues but also problems of unpredictable network disruptions in case of devices operating in remote locations. Evaluating privacy in both the paradigms is more nuanced and does not lead to a black or white result. The local processing of data, and the closeness of services to the origination of data in edge as compared to the cloud, prevents attacks which may other during the transmission of data from user to the cloud. However, the security of

**Table 2.1** Difference between cloud, fog, and edge computing

|  | Cloud computing | Fog computing | Edge computing |
|---|---|---|---|
| Architecture | Centralized | Decentralized | Decentralized |
| Data processing | On the cloud server | On the fog nodes or cloud servers | On the device |
| Analysis | Long term | Short term | Short term |
| Latency | Highest | Medium | Lowest |
| Security | Weak | Strong | Strongest |
| Operating cost | Highest | Less than or equal to cloud | Lowest |
| Connectivity | Wi-Fi | Wi-Fi, Bluetooth | Wi-Fi, Bluetooth, ZigBee, cellular connection |

individual edge devices may be weaker than the security of a cloud server, making it an easy entry point to corrupt an AI system (Ding et al., 2022).

Fog Computing, according to cisco, is an extension of the cloud computing paradigm, which brings storage and computational resources from the core of the network to the edge of the network. It facilitates the execution of applications in the edge of the network through smartly connected devices. Cloud can be thought of Even though the Fog and Edge primarily serve the same purpose of reducing latency and saving bandwidth, they differ in a few characteristics. Table 2.1 summarizes the main differences between Cloud, Fog, and Edge. The Edge Computing brings computational and storage resources closer to the user where each edge node or device partakes in processing the data. In fog computing, a decision is made by the fog nodes to either process the data through multiple terminal devices using its own resource or send it to the cloud for processing. It can also be thought of as a middle tier between the cloud server and the end device, controlling what information is sent to the cloud and what is processed locally. Moreover, various services such as IaaS, PaaS, and SaaS may be supported by Fog Computing but are not furnished by edge computing (Mukherjee et al., 2017).

## 2.4 AI TECHNIQUES FOR EDGE COMPUTING

AI is the intelligence exhibited by machines to simulate human behaviors such as reasoning, planning, thinking, problem-solving, perception, and more. Machine Learning (ML), Deep Learning (DL), Computer Vision

(CV), and Natural Language Processing (NLP) are some techniques under AI which are utilized for analyzing large datasets. Neural Networks and CV are core technologies behind various analytical computations such as voice/face recognition, image classification, video analytics, driverless cars, and the likes.

## Regression Models

Machine Learning algorithms mostly fall in the supervised learning category, where input data and their corresponding outputs are provided for the machine to learn from. Linear regression tasks are performed by finding a linear relationship between an input variable X (independent variable) and an output variable Y (independent variable). Based on this linear function, values for Y are predicted for previously unknown real-time values of X.

### Hypothesis Function of Linear Regression

$Y = \theta_0 + \theta_1 X_1 + \theta_2 X_2 + \theta_n X_n$ where, X: Input training data

$Y$: Label to the input training data or the predicted value

$\theta_0$: Intercept, i.e., bias term

$\theta_1 \ldots \theta_n$ Coefficients of X, i.e., the model parameters

The best fit line or the regression line is obtained when the error between the predicted value and the true value is minimum. Figure 2.3 depicts the best fit line in linear regression tasks. It is achieved by updating the values of $\theta_0$ and $\theta_1 \ldots \theta_n$.

**Cost Function (J)**: Cost Function (J) is the Root Mean Squared Error (RMSE) between the predicted value of y and the true value of y. It is the formal representation of a goal that the algorithm is trying to achieve. Minimizing the RMSE is accomplished through appropriate modeling and optimization techniques.

**Gradient descent**: It is an optimization algorithm which is used to minimize the sum of square of residuals (errors) by iteratively updating the values of $\theta_0$ and $\theta_1 \ldots \theta_n$. The partial derivative of the weights and biases are taken to get the slope of the cost function. The values for the weights and biases are then updated, and the process is repeated over new training data until the best fit line is achieved.

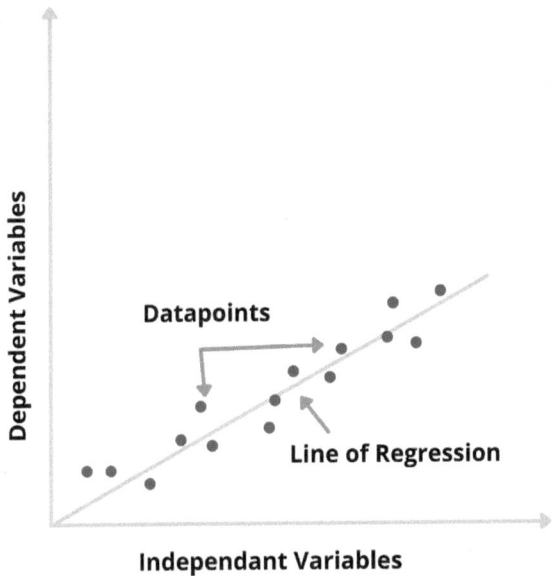

**Fig. 2.3**  Linear regression fitted line

The simplicity of linear regression makes it very versatile and scalable, and hence its use is not limited to a particular field. It is best suited for forecasting, preparing strategies according to the trends noticed, marketing effectiveness in businesses, and the likes.

### *Classification Models*

Classification models come under supervised learning, where data have predefined categories or classes. Unlike regression, the output is a category rather than a single value. The program learns from a specified data set of observations and classifies the new observations into several classes or groups. The three types of classifications include (a) Binary classification, where there are only two outcomes in this classification, e.g., yes or no, true or false; (b) multi-class classification, where there are more than two classes, and each observation or input data is mapped to a single category only; and (c) multi-label classification, where there are more than two classes, and an observation or input data is mapped to multiple categories. Based on the type of dependencies of the variables, classification algorithms can be divided into linear (Logistic Regression, Support Vector Machines) and non-linear models (K-nearest Neighbors, Kernel Support Vector Machine [SVM], Naïve Bayes, Decision Tree, and Random Forest). In this section, we will only discuss Logistic Regression and Decision Tree as they are prominently used in Edge applications but others can work well too.

**Logistic Regression**: It is a classification algorithm that uses independent variables to determine the output variable. Logistic Regression is a binary classifier and hence has only two outcomes. Its main objective is to find the best fit line for finding the best separation line between the independent and dependent variables. It is a simple algorithm that is used for spam detection, disease detection, and the likes. The two types of regression models include (a) Binary Logistic Regression Model, where the dependent variable is either of the type 0 or 1; and (b) Multinomial Logistic Regression Model, where the dependent variable can be of more than two unordered types (a type that has no quantitative significance).

**Decision Tree**: A decision tree builds classification models in a tree-like structure. The structure obtained at the end is a tree with leaf nodes and decision nodes. The decision nodes can have multiple branches, and the leaf node represents a classification. The process involves breaking down a dataset into smaller subsets and linking it with an incrementally developed decision tree. This algorithm uses sequential learning, i.e., training with one dataset at a time. The root node (i.e., the topmost node) indicates the best predictor node. Decision trees are suited for prediction analysis, data classification, and pattern recognition.

### Clustering Models

Based on unsupervised learning approach, clustering is a technique used for finding patterns, structure, and features on unlabeled datasets. Data points are grouped into clusters such that the data points in a cluster have high similarity with each other and low similarity with data points in other clusters. Many algorithms can be used for data clustering using different methods for setting similarities between data points. In this section, we will discuss some of the most popular algorithms.

**K-Means Clustering**: One of the most commonly used clustering algorithms is K-means, where n observations are divided into K clusters and K is a number already specified by the user. Each observation is grouped with the cluster having the nearest centroid to it. This approach minimizes the intra-cluster variation observed. The clustering process involves specifying a value to k, i.e., the desired number of clusters. Data points are then randomly grouped into clusters, and the centroids of the clusters are calculated. According to the Euclidean distance between the data point and its center, each data point is mapped to its nearest centroid. Finally, the mean value of data points is recalculated for each cluster and the centroids are updated. This process is iterated until the reassignment of data points to clusters terminates, indicating no more room for improvement.

**Hierarchical Clustering**: A hierarchy of clusters is built in hierarchical clustering approach. At the beginning of this approach, every data point is a cluster on its own; hence for a data set of size *n*, we will have *n* clusters. Then, the two data points or clusters closest to each other (based on the Euclidian distance) merge. The point closest to this cluster combines with it. This process is repeated until one large cluster is formed from all the sub-clusters. This approach is known as a bottom-up approach since all the clusters combine to form a single large structure. A top-down approach involves splitting up a large cluster to the point where each data point is assigned to a different cluster.

**Density-based spatial clustering of applications with noise (DBSCAN) Clustering**: Clustering is done based on the idea that clusters are a region of high point density followed by regions of low point density. The clusters formed can be of different shapes and sizes as opposed to K-means, where the clusters are of spherical shape. Figure 2.4 gives a graphical representation of DBSCAN. The two parameters considered for the formation of clusters are the threshold for the minimum numbers of points clustered together to be considered as a dense region, and a distance measure to locate points in the proximity of a particular data point. Hence, a cluster comprises of a core point which is in the center of the cluster, a border point which is near the boundary of the cluster and noise points which are present outside clusters.

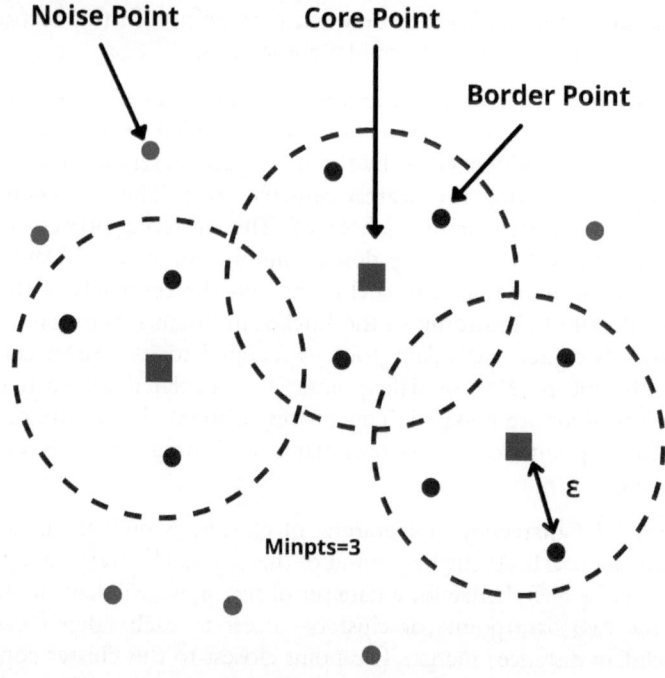

**Fig. 2.4**  Density-based spatial clustering of applications with noise

## Deep Learning and Neural Networks

Neural Networks and Deep learning models simulate the structure and working of the human brain/nervous system to precipitate cognitive abilities in machines and ultimately solve problems in image, speech, text recognition, and much more. The Artificial Neural Network (ANN) consists of a series of neurons connected to each other and arranged in multiple layers (input, middle, and output layer). To understand the working of ANNs, we need to understand the working of neurons. Perceptron, an artificial neuron, takes in several binary inputs and produces a single binary output.

The output is calculated using parameters called weights and biases. Weights are values (real numbers) associated with each input to determine the magnitude of influence each input has on the output. The weighted sum of the input, considering whether it is greater or lesser than the predefined threshold, determines the output to be either 0 or 1. The threshold taken to the left side of the inequality becomes the bias, hence if threshold is y the bias is −y.

The perceptrons are essential to understanding the basic working of neurons, but more often than not we need an output which states more than true or false (0 or 1). Moreover, the weights in a network need to be tweaked to achieve as much accuracy as possible. All the models in deep learning models also include activation functions, which are mathematically driven to predict efficient outcomes. The whole architecture of neuron and neural network is shown in Fig. 2.5.

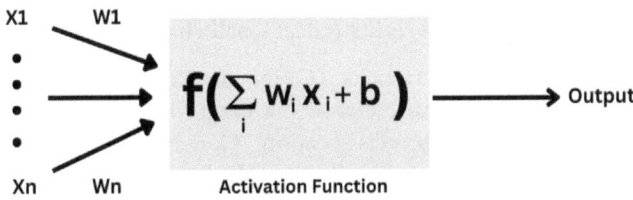

a) Working Of Artificial Neural Network

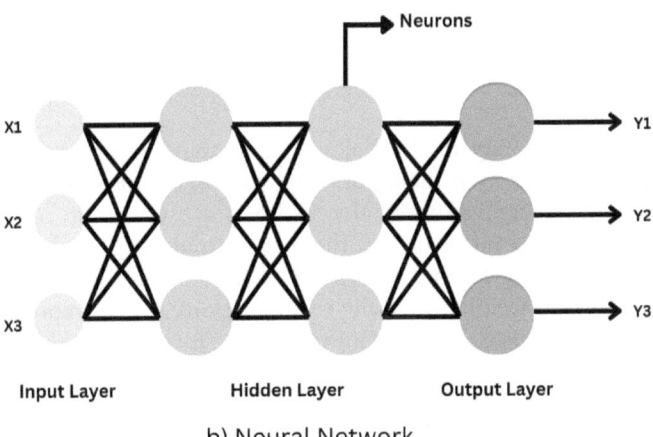

b) Neural Network

**Fig. 2.5** Structure of artificial neurons and artificial neural networks (Modified from Yu et al. [2019])

In case of a perceptron-based network, even a small change in the weights can lead to a drastic change in the output. To this end, most networks nowadays utilize the sigmoid neurons. The essential difference between perceptrons and sigmoid neurons is that instead of taking only 0 and 1 in the input, the neurons can take up any value between 0 and 1. Even the output contains a value between 0 and 1. The weights and biases perform the same role as they did with the perceptron. The output is calculated using the sigma function. The working of sigmoid neuron is very similar to the perceptron: if the value in the output is a number closer to 1, we can assume the output to be true. If the output is closer to 0 we can assume the output to be false. The graph of the function is smooth, rather than sharp as in the case of perceptrons, which indicates that small changes in the weights reflect small changes in the output.

**Convolution Neural Networks (CNN or ConvNet):** CNNs are a special type of Deep Neural Networks, known for performing computer vision tasks such as image classification. ConvNet requires much less pre-processing compared to shallower Machine Learning algorithms. Primitive methods require manual filter development, but ConvNet has the ability to learn these filters through the training process. The input provided to the CNN is generally two-dimensional (e.g., matrix of pixels) mapped to an output variable after applying a series of filters in the convolution layer. The architecture of ConvNet comprises three the convolution layer, pooling layer and, the fully connected layer.

a. **Convolution Layer**: The majority of computations take place in the convolution layer. If the input is an image in the form of a 3D matrix of pixels depicting the height, width, and RGB value of image, a filter or kernel moves across the matrix to identify a particular part of the target object in the image. The filter or feature detector is also a matrix (of weights), usually of dimensions $3 \times 3$, representing a part of the image that we want to identify, for example, the top horizontal line of the number 5. The dot product is calculated between the filter and an input pixel which is known as a convolution operation and the result is placed on the feature map. The filter is then shifted by a stride value and the process is repeated.

b. **Pooling Layer**: The pooling layer reduces the size of the feature maps as well as overfitting as there are less parameters to learn. It summarizes the features, using either max pooling or average pooling, in a region of the feature map. Additional operations are then performed on the summed features instead of the exactly placed features generated by the convolutional layer. This makes the CNN more robust to position changes in the image. The two types of pooling methods used are max pooling and average pooling. In max pooling, the filter takes the maximum element from a part of the feature map, shifts by its stride value, and repeats the process until it sweeps across the entire feature map, generating an output array consisting essentially of the prominent features. Average pooling, which is not often used, takes the average of the features and stores it in the output array.

c. **Fully Connected Layer**: In the convolution layer each input node is not connected to each and every output node, and hence it is a partially connected layer. However, the fully connected layer is a normal feed-forward neural network where each node in output layer is connected to a node in the previous layer. The input to this layer is the output from the final pooling or convolution layer which is flattened and fed into the fully connected neural network. The convolution and pooling layers generally use a Rectified Linear Unit (ReLU) activation function to introduce non-linearity to the model, while the fully connected layer uses a softmax activation function to perform classification tasks based on the features extracted from the convolution layer.

**Popular Convolution Neural Networks**: AlexNet (Krizhevsky et al., 2012) won the ImageNet LSVRC-2010 contest by classifying 1.2 million high-resolution images into 1000 categories, achieving top-1 and top-5 error rates of 37.5% and 17.0%. The model has 60 million parameters, 650,000 neurons, and its architecture comprises five convolution layers (some followed by pooling layers) and three fully connected layers ending with a 1000-way softmax. The first use of the non-linearity function ReLu, was seen in this neural network. This model is also characterized by heavy data augmentation, excellent implementation of GPUs, non-saturating neurons, and the use of dropout 0.5 to reduce overfitting. In 2014, VGGNet (Simonyan & Zisserman, 2014) won the first and second places in localization and classification tracks respectively of the ImageNet challenge. As compared to AlexNet, VGG has a total of 138 million parameters and significantly more depth in the network, consisting of 16 and 19 layers, respectively, in their VGG-16 and VGG-19 variants.

This model utilizes small filters ($3 \times 3$) with stride 1, and a stack of three of these filters gives the same effective receptive field as one $7 \times 7$ filter. The motivation for smaller filters is the lesser number of parameters per layer, as well as more depth which introduces more non-linearity. They also mention in their work that the fully connected layer (consisting of 4096 channels), which lies just before the layer which goes into 1000 ImageNet classes, is sufficient to extract features from data and generalize to other tasks. GoogleNet (Szegedy et al., 2015) outperforms both AlexNet and VGGNet in terms of accuracy as well as the architecture layout. Being deeper, and more computationally efficient, it achieved 6.7% top 5 error and won the ILSVRC'14 classification challenge. The architecture consists of some convolution and fooling layers in the beginning, followed by a stack of inception modules, and finally a classifier output which does not consist of any fully connected layers. The removal of these FC layers allows for only the network to be trained using only 5 million parameters which is $12\times$ less than the parameters used in AlexNet. The inception modules significantly improve computational efficiency as parallel convolution and pooling operations are applied on the same input. The results of these operations are concatenated and the tensor output produced serves as the input for the next inception module. The operations tend to be computationally very expensive and also the pooling layer preserves the depth of the features. Hence, the total depth can only be increased at each layer after concatenation. To this end, $1 \times 1$ convolutions are used as dimension reduction modules to remove computation bottlenecks. In addition, they serve as dual-purpose modules as they also include the use of ReLU function, adding depth and non-linearity to the network. The SqueezeNet architecture (Landola et al., 2016) uses a Fire module consisting of a "squeeze" layer with a $1 \times 1$ filter that feeds into an "expand" layer that contains both $1 \times 1$ and $3 \times 3$ filters. Using 50 $\times$ fewer parameters than AlexNet, SqueezeNet is still able to achieve the same level of accuracy and leveraging model compression techniques it can compress to $510\times$ smaller than AlexNet.

**Recurrent Neural Networks (RNN)**: RNNs use sequential data feeding where the basic unit of the models is a cell comprising of layers (input, middle, and output). A series of connected units(cells) perform the sequential processing of RNN models. They are widely used for natural language processing and speech recognition. RNNs primarily work on the principle of processing each input sequence by iterating over each of its elements and remembering the state that stores the information as per the already seen/retrieved information. The state of RNN is reset between processing two different but independent sequences (Chollet, 2021). LSTM and GRU are popular RNN techniques which are iterative in nature.

## 2.5   SUMMARY

This chapter lays the groundwork for understanding EdgeAI by explaining its two crucial components individually, namely Edge Computing and Artificial Intelligence. Firstly, we introduce edge computing along with a brief summary of some related terms such as Mobile Edge Computing, Cloudlet, and Fog Computing. Next, we review some AI use cases (smart city, online shopping, video analytics, and smart fitness watches), which best help to highlight the motivation and benefits of edge computing. We then provide a comparative analysis of cloud, fog, and edge paradigms to give better clarity on the differences between all three architectures This is followed by a holistic view of AI models with a special emphasis on Deep Neural Networks. We briefly discuss regression models, clustering models (K-means clustering, hierarchical clustering, and DBSCAN) and classification models (Logistic regression and binary tree) before moving on to Deep Learning and Deep Neural Networks. In the following sections where we review EdgeAI and its use cases, we mainly talk about DNNs at the edge; hence we provide a thorough account of Deep Learning concepts, models, and popular frameworks in this chapter. Firstly, we talk about the concepts of gradient descent, activation functions and loss functions, and the basic working of basic Artificial Neural Networks. We then move on to Convolution Neural Networks popularly used for image classification, computer vision tasks, and object recognition. Lastly, we review the working of Recurrent Neural Networks, commonly used for Natural Language Processing seen in chatbots and intelligent agents such as Apple's Siri or Google's voice search.

# REFERENCES

Alpaydin, E. (2021). *Machine learning*. MIT Press.

Chollet, F. (2021). *Deep learning with Python*. Simon and Schuster.

Cisco Fog Computing Solutions. (2015). *Unleash the power of the Internet of Things*. Cisco Systems Inc.

Ding, A. Y., Peltonen, E., Meuser, T., Aral, A., Becker, C., Dustdar, S., Hiessl, T., Kranzlmüller, D., Liyanage, M., Magshudi, S., Mohan, N., Ott, J., Rellermeyer, J. S., Schulte, S., Schulzrinne, H., Solmaz, G., Tarkoma, S., Varghese, B., & Wolf, L. (2022). Roadmap for Edge AI: A Dagstuhl perspective. *ACM SIGCOMM Computer Communication Review, 52*(1), 28–33.

Goodfellow, I., Bengio, Y., & Courville, A. (2016). *Deep learning*. MIT Press.

Iandola, F. N., Han, S., Moskewicz, M. W., Ashraf, K., Dally, W. J., & Keutzer, K. (2016). *SqueezeNet: AlexNet-level accuracy with 50x fewer parameters and <0.5 MB model size*. arXiv preprint arXiv: https://arxiv.org/abs/1602.07360

Krizhevsky, A., Sutskever, I., & Hinton, G. E. (2012). Imagenet classification with deep convolutional neural networks. *Advances in Neural Information Processing Systems, 25*, 1097–1105.

Mukherjee, M., Matam, R., Shu, L., Maglaras, L., Ferrag, M. A., Choudhury, N., & Kumar, V. (2017). Security and privacy in fog computing: Challenges. *IEEE Access, 5*, 19293–19304.

Rumelhart, D. E., Hinton, G. E., & Williams, R. J. (1986). Learning representations by back-propagating backerrors. *Nature, 323*(6088), 533–536.

Satyanarayanan, M., Bahl, P., Caceres, R., & Davies, N. (2009). The case for vm-based cloudlets in mobile computing. *IEEE Pervasive Computing, 8*(4), 14–23.

Schmidhuber, J. (2015). Deep learning in neural networks: An overview. *Neural Networks, 61*, 85–117.

Simonyan, K., & Zisserman, A. (2014). *Very deep convolutional networks for large-scale image recognition*. arXiv preprint arXiv: https://arxiv.org/abs/1409.1556

Szegedy, C., Liu, W., Jia, Y., Sermanet, P., Reed, S., Anguelov, D., Erhan, D., Vanhoucke, V., & Rabinovich, A. (2015). Going deeper with convolutions. In *Proceedings of the IEEE conference on computer vision and pattern recognition* (pp. 1–9).

Yi, S., Hao, Z., Qin, Z., & Li, Q. (2015, November). Fog computing: Platform and applications. In *2015 Third IEEE workshop on hot topics in web systems and technologies (HotWeb)* (pp. 73–78). IEEE.

Yu, Y., Hur, T., Jung, J., & Jang, I. G. (2019). Deep learning for determining a near-optimal topological design without any iteration. *Structural and Multidisciplinary Optimization, 59*, 787–799. https://doi.org/10.1007/s00158-018-2101-5

# CHAPTER 3

# EdgeAI: Concept and Architecture

**Abstract** In this chapter, we introduce the concept of EdgeAI, followed by a brief talk on how AI benefits edge computing and vice versa. We then move to discuss the variety of architectures that may be adopted for implementing AI at the edge, explicitly elaborating on training and inference architectures separately. Next, we provide a holistic view of the different criteria to evaluate the processes of Model Training and Model Inference at the edge. We then review emerging frameworks and technologies which assist the training and inference processes by targeting and improving specific Key Performance Indicators (KPIs). We also analyze how each enabling technology impacts the different KPIS for both the training and inference process. Finally, we summarize all the architectures, criteria for evaluating AI model workflow, and the enabling technologies for model training and inference at the edge in the form of a comparative analysis.

**Keywords** EdgeAI · Model training · Model inference · Architectures · Enabling technologies · Key Performance Indicators

© The Author(s), under exclusive license to Springer Nature Singapore Pte Ltd. 2023
R. Gupta et al., *EdgeAI for Algorithmic Government*, https://doi.org/10.1007/978-981-19-9798-3_3

## 3.1    Concept

Government decisions affect the country as a whole and its reputation and standing in the international arena. Moreover, public services require a lot of personnel and resources to cater to the entire nation's needs. For example, in 2016, the United States Social Security Administration (SSA) received 2.5 billion disability claims, and 700,000 appeals were filed at the hearing level (Engstrom et al., 2020). The waiting time for a hearing can vary from several months to more than two years. By leveraging AI, cases are processed faster, and even the wait time for the hearing has been shortened, as applicants expected to receive benefits are moved forward in the queue. In addition, security commissions and exchanges received financial statements from more than 7,000 issuers (Engstrom et al., 2020), requiring extensive verification by the agent's limited staff. The adoption of Corporate Issuer Risk Assessment, which utilizes machine learning tools to seek through the data, anomaly detection, and misconduct prediction, has become a breeze, leading to an efficient workflow for the agency. Therefore, algorithms facilitating large-scale government decision-making processes and public services must be well structured, secure, and fast, resulting in transparent and righteous governance. The cloud-centric architecture of AI is no longer suitable for the rapid calculations and analysis that must be performed on such a massive volume of data. To this end, we need to bring the computing services closer to the user devices, i.e., at the edge of the network. This complimentary relationship of Edge Computing and AI is what we call EdgeAI or Edge Intelligence (Lovén et al., 2019), which aims to realize the potential benefits of AI at the network edge instead of the network core. In the previous chapter, we have covered the basics of Edge computing. In this chapter we will focus on artificial intelligence concept and architectures inside the Edge Computing.

## 3.2    EdgeAI Approaches

Edge is known for its distributed paradigm, which enables data processing close to the user/data-generating devices, and AI helps perform intelligent tasks by learning from the data. It is evident that they both complement each other, and the fusion of both leads to many benefits for both edge computing and AI.

**AI For Edge**: AI for Edge involves the deployment of AI paradigms such as reasoning, predictive data analysis, intelligent agents, and more to solve the optimization problems of edge computing. With the proliferation of IoT devices, humongous amounts of data are sensed by the edge devices continuously. Therefore, predictive data analysis is required to enable real-time decision-making in IoT applications like traffic control, border patrol using drones, disaster prevention, and the likes. Hence, AI is needed to quickly analyze complex tasks and perform intelligent mining on the regularly churned data. Applications utilizing face recognition or real-time video analytics which require continuous, high-quality data with low latency and high privacy work perfectly in the edge environment. Hence, edge can be popularized with these AI applications. Moreover, an edge infrastructure is shared by multiple actors which work together to meet their individual exacting demands. This distributed architecture leads to several decision-makers instead of one central decision-maker, and can also engender conflict of interests among various actors. AI helps optimize the orchestration of edge's decentralized architecture by helping the various actors interact and learn to make decisions together and also by handling low throughput and resource-allocation issues. It also enhances edge security by detecting anomalies in the network connection and providing autonomous, location-aware personalized systems to each user.

**Edge For AI**: Apart from the usual benefits of AI models at the edge (including low latency, reduced bandwidth/power consumption, and increased scalability and reliability), edge provides AI with rich application data, scenarios, and model parameters as a result of the data generated by IoT devices at the edge. Hence, the performance of AI models will improve as they will have a richer data set to train from. As the processing of data is happening locally, not only is Edge helping in timeliness and responsiveness but also in reducing privacy leakages as the data no longer has to travel to the central cloud. Moreover, edge is needed to democratize AI. Ubiquitous AI or AI Democratization is a concept that is gaining a lot of popularity. It is the idea of making intelligent machines and systems accessible to everyone. To spread the base of AI to a larger audience, we need to push the AI frontiers closer to the user devices. To this end, Edge is a better option than the cloud architecture.

## 3.3    ARCHITECTURE OF EDGE INTELLIGENCE

Training and inference of AI models are generally assumed to be done on the cloud because of the intensive computations and resources required for both. However, this comes at the cost of privacy leakages and communication latency, both of which are non-negligible Key Performance Indicators (KPIs). Hence, the full scope of Edge Intelligence fully leverages the data and resources available in the edge network, user devices, and cloud data centers to optimize the AI workflows for the models. According to the location of training and inference of AI model, and the amount of data offloading, Edge Intelligence (EI) has been categorized into six levels by Zhou et al. (2019).

a. **Cloud architecture**: Training and Inference of the model takes place in the cloud. This is suited for larger and more complex models which require intensive resources and computation. However, it invokes the issues of communication latencies and privacy leakages and therefore is not the most efficient.

b. **Level 1—Training in the cloud and inference in an Edge-Cloud collaboration**: In this level, training of the model takes place on the cloud, and inferencing is done in an edge-cloud synergy, meaning some of the resources are offloaded to the cloud. Communication across the edge and cloud can cause latency and privacy issues.

c. **Level 2—Training in the cloud and inference in the network Edge**: Here, an AI model is trained on the cloud, and inferencing is done at the edge (a single edge node, server, or the entire edge network). Therefore, energy consumption, communication latency, and memory footprint are key challenges to consider.

d. **Level 3—Training on the cloud and inference on the device**: In this level, the model is trained on the cloud, and inferencing is done on the device itself. However, since end devices are resource and energy-constrained, Energy efficiency, memory footprint, and accuracy cannot be ruled out.

e. **Level 4—Training and Inference in an Edge-Cloud collaboration: This level corresponds to the** training and inferencing of the model facilitated by edge-cloud cooperation. This brings in a lot of communication overhead and also risks privacy leakage.

f. **Level 5—Training and Inference in the network Edge**: Training and inferencing of the AI model takes place at the edge. Energy efficiency and communication latency across the edge network are some challenges to consider.

g. **Level 6—Training and Inference on the device**: The AI model training and inference take place entirely on the device. Since these are resource-hungry tasks that consume a lot of energy, consideration of memory footprint, energy efficiency, and accuracy is vital.

## *Training Specific Architectures*

The AI workflow's model training or building process requires tremendous amounts of training data and processing power. With its enormous computational resources and storage and processing capacity, cloud seems perfect for the task. However, the problems of latency, privacy, and communication cost cannot be ignored. Edge provides the solution to these problems by reducing bandwidth consumption and privacy leakages and improving the scalability and latency of the models. Hence, this section will review the key architectures that enable the distributed training of AI models to improve their general performance.

a. **Centralized Architecture**: Data from various remote terminal devices such as phones, smart watches, environmental sensors, etc., are acquired and sent to the cloud. The AI model training is then performed in the cloud leveraging these data (Calo et al., 2017). This architecture is considered useful when the model is too large and complex or when the data needs a single homogenous environment to be trained (e.g., Clustering Models). Since training of the model takes place in the cloud, it covers the cloud intelligence, level 1, level 2, and level 3 of the aforementioned EI levels.

b. **Decentralized Architecture**: In AI-based IoT solutions like multi-agent systems, where the different systems interact with each other in an intricate manner and are inherently distributed, the centralized architecture may not be the best solution (Calo et al., 2017; Yang et al., 2021). Hence, a decentralized edge topology, e.g., a tree-like structure, is favored in these situations. E-Tree and Gossip training are some paradigms that complement this mode of training. Figure 3.1 gives an overview of the centralized, decentralized, and hybrid architectures. In this architecture, each node or terminal device maintains some of the model parameters and trains the model on its local data. All the local model updates are then aggravated by exchanging information among the various edge nodes through network connections (Chang et al., 2022) to obtain the global model. There is no dependence on a central node; hence it can be identified with EI level 5.

c. **Hybrid Architecture**: It is the fusion between decentralized and centralized architecture. Federated Learning, an EI approach to preserve privacy, is based on hybrid architecture. In this architecture, the terminal devices train the AI models by exchanging decentralized updates with each other, which are then combined and sent to a central edge server or a cloud server. The central server optimizes the global model and sends the updated model parameters back to the edge devices. This architecture can correspond to EI levels 4 and 5.

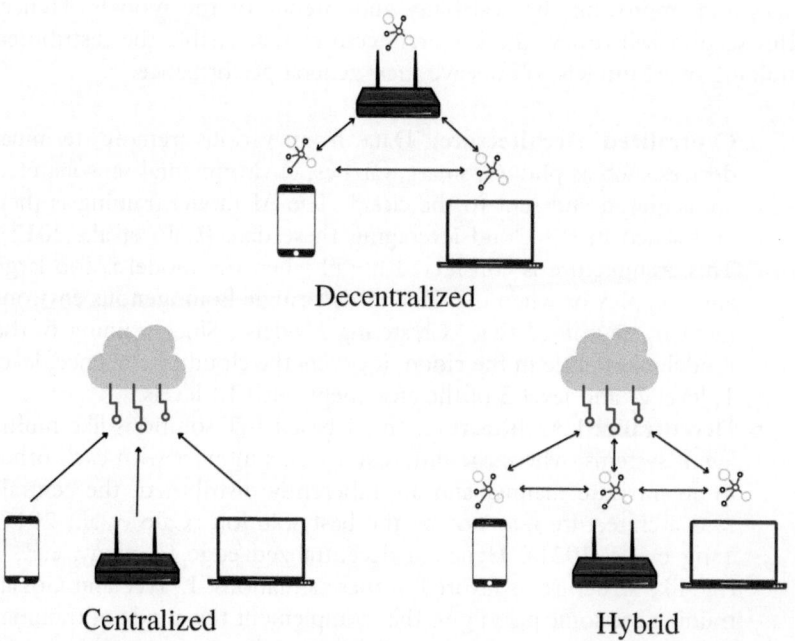

Decentralized

Centralized                                Hybrid

**Fig. 3.1**   Centralized, decentralized, and hybrid architectures for model training at the edge

*Inference Specific Architectures*

Some use cases of IoT applications, like border patrol using drones, require quick response time, which cannot be achieved if the data is sent to the cloud for inference. Figure 3.1 gives an overview of the four inference specific architectures. This section reviews architectures which enable model inference at the edge.

a. **On Edge Inference**: In this architecture, input data from remote terminal devices are sent to a central edge server for inference, and the results obtained are sent back to the devices. Since the model inference occurs at the server, it is highly scalable. However, inference is highly dependent on the available bandwidth and network connection quality between the edge server and the user devices.

b. **On Device Inference**: In this architecture, a terminal device obtains the trained model from the edge server, and executes the model on the device itself. Since the device is not dependent on a central server, it is very reliable. Challenges can arise in this mode due to the restrictions caused by the resource deprived devices. Hence, the inference process should be energy efficient.

c. **Edge-Device co-inference**: Such architecture means that the AI model is divided and distributed among the edge devices and the server for inference. Simple computations are executed on the device, and the processed data is sent to an edge server for completing the inference process. This architecture is, therefore, reliable and versatile. Furthermore, privacy is preserved since part of the model parameters deployed on the device and servers, eliminating data exposure. However, the arduous process of inference can cause stress on resource-constrained devices.

d. **Edge-Cloud co-inference**: When enormous resources and intensive computations are required, inference occurs in edge-cloud cooperation. The data is collected from the user devices themselves. Therefore, available bandwidth and the reliability of the connection highly influence the performance of model inference (Fig. 3.2).

## 3.4   Evaluating AI Model Workflow at Edge

Key Performance Indicators (KPIs) are critical performance measures which help in evaluating the performance of the training and inference of models across the aforementioned architectures. The main KPIs for Edge AI are described below.

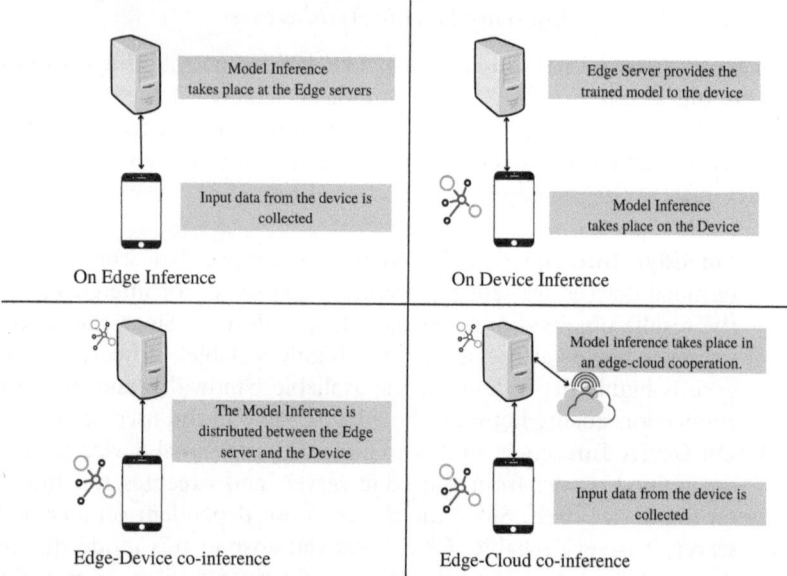

**Fig. 3.2**  Edge-based, device-based, edge-device, and edge-cloud architectures for model inference at the edge

1. **Latency**: Generally, Latency or delay in the context of an application refers to transmission/communication/computation latency. The latter is tightly dependent on the computation capacity of the server or system. Typically, applications are deployed on terminal IoT devices which are circumscribed in terms of computational power. In these situations, the data generated by IoT devices can be uploaded to the cloud to give full play to its primacy of storage and computational capacity. However, the transmission of data from the network edge to the cloud can lead to considerable transmission delay. Hence, determining the trade-off between computation and transmission delay to ensure the efficacy of applications is crucial. When we talk about model training, the latency of training directly determines when the model is ready for use. Specifically, the computation latency depends upon hardware, software, and the

edge device's potential in general whereas the communication or transmission latency is determined by the size of input data, available bandwidth, and transmission method. For model inference, latency refers to the duration taken for the inference process and relies upon the transmission method, available bandwidth, and resources present on the edge device. Many applications have strict latency requirements (e.g., under 5 ms for 5G cellular data), and hence latency is an essential criterion to consider.

2. **Overhead/Communication Cost**: The plethora of data packets (containing header overhead and payload) generated by user devices introduces a lot of transmission overhead. Communication cost generally arises from the transference of data and resources across the edge network. In the case of distributed training, where the various nodes of a network work collaboratively to train a model, communication overhead is inevitable. And this, in turn, increases bandwidth, energy/power consumption, and latency. Overhead is essentially dependent on the volume of raw input data, available bandwidth, and the transmission method. Overhead during inference is caused by the decentralization execution of the model. The on-device inference architecture is an exception since the model is executed entirely on the device. Therefore, here communication cost mainly depends on the available bandwidth and the architecture used for inference.

3. **Privacy**: This is a very important criterion, especially for EdgeAI applications, which offer both ways to improve trust, security, and privacy, but also adds challenges. In an edge network, the data generated are either processed on the terminal devices themselves or on edge servers which are in close proximity to them. This data locality helps to increase security; however, it is wrong to assume that the privacy of edge is higher than cloud just because of the locality of data. The distributed nature of edge involving various actors elicits trust issues within the system, and consequently, the trust of edge nodes is more challenging to maintain than cloud providers. During model training, it should be made sure that the more privacy sensitive data is processed on the device and the less privacy sensitive data is offloaded to the edge or cloud. The realization of privacy protection hence depends on whether the raw data is sent to the edge for processing or not. Similarly, privacy-sensitive

data generated by user devices need to be handled carefully during the inference of the AI model. Privacy preservation is especially crucial in healthcare, military, finance, and other similar applications. In the case of inference, where privacy preservation is implemented or not depends on the method of processing the raw data.

4. **Energy**: The entire AI model workflow is an arduous and taxing process that is typically suitable for the high computing and storage capacity of cloud centers. The power constrained terminal devices do not fit with the energy draining training process of models. Therefore, the AI model should be designed to be energy efficient. The size of the resources used and the complexity of the training model are factors that affect energy efficiency. Similarly, the communication and computation overhead during model inference tends to be energy exhaustive which is unsuitable for the battery-limited edge devices. Hence, the preservation and management of energy are essential to optimize AI inference. Energy efficiency is mainly dependent on the resources (hardware/software) available on terminal devices and the size of the AI model.

5. **Accuracy**: Accuracy of an AI model is a quantitative measure to indiciate if a model is working well and fulfilling its intended purpose in a correct manner. Hence, it is a criterion specific for model inference, not model training. It can be defined as the number of samples predicted correctly to the total number of samples to be predicted. EI Applications such as Autonomous Vehicles and Face Recognition for criminal detection require ultra-high accuracy. Accuracy for inference at the edge is especially a crucial evaluating metric; for applications such as video analytics, continuous High-definition footage is sensed at the edge, and some frames may be dropped to ensure quick real-time analysis, leading to low accuracy (Zhou et al., 2019). Here, the speed of input being fed to the could be a determining factor for accuracy. Accuracy is a fundamental performance metric as it directly evaluates the performance of the inference process.

6. **Memory Footprint**: Typically, AI models consist of a myriad of parameters. They are designed to run on hardware such as multi core processors, CPUs, or GPU with high-bandwidth dedicated memory, all of which are provided by the powerful and robust cloud data centers. At the edge, the resource-constrained devices do not provide a dedicated memory bandwidth for device GPUs and CPUs

leading them to fight for the scarce resources. Hence, memory footprint, which can be defined as the amount of main memory referred to by an application while running, is an important KPI for model inference which requires a lot of resources from mobile devices. It depends on the size of the AI model and the way of loading the parameters accompanied by AI models.

## 3.5   Enabling Technologies for Improving KPIs

In this section we review novel enabling technologies and frameworks which help in optimizing the aforementioned KPIs in the context of EI model training and model inferencing.

### Enabling Technologies for Model Training

The ML model training process includes providing training data for ML algorithms, from which the model learns. The labeled data contains input already mapped to the target output (correct output). The ML algorithms learn from the sampled data by finding patterns in it. Training an AI model involves fitting good weights and biases to the ML algorithm. Initially, random values of weights are assigned to the input. A loss function determines how far the predictions are from the true label. Using the backpropagation mechanism, the generated error rate is transmitted back across the entire network, and the values of weights are updated according to that. Until the error rate is below a certain threshold, the backpropagation process is repeated, and new input samples are fed to the neural network to achieve high accuracy. So far, we have discussed the relevant architectures used to facilitate the training process and the Key Performance Indicators used to evaluate the performance of Model Training. Table 3.1 shows the impact of different Enabling Technologies on KPIs for EI model training. Below, we have summarized apposite Enabling Technologies, which help improve the KPIs mentioned above.

a. **Federated Learning or Collaborative Learning**
   Each edge device contributes to some part of the dataset required for training a model. Traditional approaches collected the data from all the devices and sent it to the cloud for training, making the data vulnerable to privacy leakages. To this end McMahan et al.

**Table 3.1** Impact of enabling technologies on KPIs for EI model training

| Correlation | Communication cost | Privacy | Latency | Energy efficiency |
|---|---|---|---|---|
| Federated learning | Low | High | High | Medium |
| Aggregation frequency control | High | Medium | High | Medium |
| Gradient compression | High | Low | Medium | Medium |
| Model splitting | Low | High | Medium | Medium |
| Knowledge transfer learning | Low | Medium | Low | High |
| Gossip training | Low | Medium | High | Medium |
| E-tree | High | Low | High | Medium |

(2017) propose Federated Learning, an approach where a model is trained across distributed edge devices without exchanging the data between them. The local training data on a client is not shared with any other client or server. Instead, local updates are computed on each client and aggravated by a central server to reach a global model. For this purpose, FederatedAveraging (FedAvg) is proposed (McMahan et al., 2017) where stochastic gradient descent (SGD) is applied on each client combined with iterative model averaging done by a server. Optimization and communication are some challenges of federated learning as each device has to send model updates after local training, thus increasing the communication overhead. FedAvg considers unbalanced and non-independent identical distribution (non-IID) data and focuses on reducing the communication rounds, thereby decreasing the communication cost. As computations take place locally on the datasets present at each device, privacy is also optimized considerably. However, the communication process in FedAvg is time-consuming, and the edge devices are required to perform many computations. To counter these problems, (Ye et al., 2020) propose EdgeFed algorithm, which leverages a client-edge-cloud architecture. The model updates are performed between the client and edge server, taking advantage of the high bandwidth and low latency. The intensive computations are offloaded to the edge serves, leaving the client devices to train the lower layers of the model. The global aggregation is done in edge-cloud collaboration, reducing the communication cost while reaching threshold accuracy required for proper training of the model.

b. **Aggregation Frequency Control**

Gradient-descent-based Federated Learning includes each node performing a one-step SGD to minimize the loss function on its training dataset. An iterative global aggregation step is also executed where the adjusted local model parameters from every client is sent to a remote aggregator which takes the weighted average of the parameters and sends it back to the nodes. However, the local updates calculated drain the computation resources of clients while the global aggregation step increases the communication overhead of the entire network. Therefore, we need to carefully control the aggregation process, including the aggregation content and the aggregation frequency, considering the constraint on resources on edge devices and the unreliable and limited bandwidth for global updates aggregation. Wang et al. (2019) proposed a control algorithm that learns the data distribution, system dynamics, and model characteristics by analyzing the convergence bound of gradient-descent-based federated learning from a theoretical perspective, and obtaining a novel convergence bound that incorporates non-IID data distribution among nodes and an arbitrary number of local updates between two global aggregations. This algorithm automatically adjusts global aggregate frequencies in real time to minimize loss in learning within a fixed resource budget. This method focuses on reducing and improving communication overhead during distributed training of DNN models.

c. **Gradient Compression**

Compression of model updates is required to reduce the communication overhead in decentralized training of models. Gradient quantization and gradient sparsification are two methods that are used to compress model updates (Shi et al., 2020; Zhou et al., 2019). Gradient quantization refers to quantizing the elements of the gradient vectors to a finite-bit low precision value instead of a 32-bit floating-point value (lossy compression). Gradient sparsification transmits only the important gradient vectors (decided by some criteria) to reduce communication overhead.

d. **Model Splitting or Model Partition**

Model partitioning is performed on AI models, when the model size is too large to be trained on a resource-constrained edge node.

The AI model can be internally partitioned between two consecutive layers with the two divisions deployed on different locations without any loss in accuracy (Shi et al., 2020). Keeping the latency requirement in mind, the main challenge is figuring out where to split the model (Zhou et al., 2019). At the edge of the network, a model is deployed across distributed edge devices or across an edge device and an edge or cloud server, with each device holding a part of model parameters and computing its respective updates to train the model collaboratively. However, model partitioning increases the communication cost due to the collaborative nature of training and the performance of models as the data sent to the edge or cloud server from the device is often distorted to preserve privacy. To combat these challenges, Wang et al. (2018) proposed privAte infeRence framework based on Deep nEural Networks, a framework which targets preserving privacy and improving performance of model. DNN model is split between a device and the cloud, where the device holds shallow layers of the model to transform the raw data and the cloud holds larger and complex parts of the model to tackle computation- and resource-intensive tasks. Arden uses a differential privacy mechanism on the device side, adding random noise to the data before uploading it to the cloud which not only preserves privacy but also improves the robustness of DNN model.

e. **Knowledge Transfer Learning**

In this approach, a teacher or base network is first trained on a base data set, and the acquired characteristics/functionalities are passed on to a student network which is then trained on a target data set. This dramatically decreases resource consumption and optimizes energy efficiency since the knowledge gained from a previously trained model is reused on another model. This approach can be applied only when the two tasks (base task and student task) are similar (Zhou et al., 2019). Sharma et al. (2018) provide an extensive study to evaluate the performance of Knowledge Transfer Learning against different transferring techniques and architectures. The best performance is observed when knowledge is transferred from the middle layers as well as the last year of the base model to the student model. Some architectures and techniques even lead to a bad impact on the accuracy and convergence speed of the training models.

#### f. Gossip Training

In distributed training of the model, models are trained locally, and the weighted average of the updates is computed by a central server. However, Gossip Training allows for a fully decentralized manner of training, where devices exchange information with each other to collaboratively train a model without depending on a central server. Hence, reaching a fast consensus (obtaining the global model) by exchanging local updates with various edge nodes (gossiping) is essential to reduce training latency (Shi et al., 2020; Zhou et al., 2019). Gossip Algorithms at the edge also benefit from asynchronization as there is no dependence on a central server. To speed up the training process of DNNs, Blot et al. (2016) proposed Gossip Stochastic Gradient Descent algorithm (GoSGD) where each node contains the DNN model. The algorithm works iteratively consisting of two phases—gradient update and mixing update. In the gradient update step, each node uses SGD to update the model and in the mixing step, the nodes exchange information with a randomly selected node.

#### g. E-Tree

E-Tree is a distributed learning approach used to group edge devices, leveraging intelligent clustering algorithms called K-Means and Average Accuracy (KMA), based on the distribution of data across different edge devices and the network distance between devices. (Yang et al., 2021). The structure of the E-tree comprises a bottom layer of leaf nodes which are essentially model learning edge devices (Calo et al., 2017). Non-leaf nodes depict the model aggregation. The leaf nodes train the models locally with their data set, and an internal node collects those aggregated updates and sends back the updated model to the children nodes. The tree structure is made such that parallelism is maximized and the communication cost and latency are reduced.

Table 3.1 shows correlation matrix represents the positive and negative impacts an Enabling technology has on one or more of the key performance indicators for EI Model Training.

## Enabling Technologies for Model Inference

After the model is trained, the inference phase begins. Machine Learning inference refers to a testing of the model to predict output for previously unforeseen data. For example, after a model is trained to recognize certain target objects from images, for an image classification application, it is fed novel images from real time to make predictions out of them or to classify them. Unlike the training process, ML inference consists of only the feed-forward process, not the backpropagation process. So far, we have discussed the relevant architectures used to facilitate the inference process and the criteria used to evaluate the performance of Model Inference. Table 3.2 shows the impact of different Enabling Technologies on KPIs for EI model inference. Below, we have summarized apposite Enabling Technologies, which help improve the KPIs mentioned above.

a. **Model Compression**

Edge devices like cellphones and sensors are resource-constrained, and hence device-based inference of largely dense over-parametrized DNN models is rarely possible. This introduces latency and privacy issues. Thus, model compression is done to simplify and reduce

**Table 3.2**   Impact of enabling technologies on KPIs for EI model inference

| Correlation | Accuracy | Privacy | Latency | Energy | Memory footprint | Communication overhead |
|---|---|---|---|---|---|---|
| Model compression | Low | High | High | High | High | Medium |
| Model partition | Low | High | High | High | Medium | Medium |
| Model early exit | Medium | Medium | High | Medium | Medium | Medium |
| Edge caching | Medium | Low | High | Medium | Medium | Medium |
| Input filtering | Medium | Low | High | High | Medium | Low |
| Model selection | High | Low | High | High | Low | Low |
| Support for multitenancy | Medium | Low | Medium | Low | High | High |
| Application specific optimization | High | Low | High | High | High | Medium |

the size of AI models to optimize their storage and allow device-based inference. This also reduces the number of resources required from the end devices and optimizes energy and memory footprint. The commonly adopted techniques in model compression are weight pruning and data quantization. Quantization helps compress the model by representing the weights or the inputs with a more compact format rather than a 32-bit floating-point format. Gong et al. (2014) review various vector quantization methods, and it is found that applying simple K-means clustering or product quantization to weights gives commendable results as compared to conventional mixed factorization methods. They achieve 16–24 times CNN-network compression for the ImageNet challenge with just 1% loss in classification accuracy. Another commonly used technique, pruning, removes redundant weights or connections between neurons from a trained model. Han et al. (2015) propose a three-step pruning method keeping in mind the resource limited hardware. The first step involves learning the essential connections in the model. In the second step, redundant and unimportant weights are removed, and in the last step, the remaining weights are fine-tuned to preserve the model accuracy. This method yielded brilliant results for AlexNet and VGG-16, where the size of both the networks reduced drastically, by $35\times$ and $49\times$ respectively, without incurring any loss in accuracy.

b. **Model Partition**

To accelerate the execution of complex models and ease the pressure on resource-constrained end devices, the AI model is partitioned between various devices or between a device and an edge server (Shi et al., 2020). The computation-intensive and resource-exhaustive processes are mainly done in the server, reducing the energy and latency cost. Since the model parameters are distributed among the devices and the edge serve, the exposure of user data is also reduced (Zhou et al., 2019). The main challenge is deciding the partitioning point to optimize the inference process. Mao et al. (2017) devise a partition method in their mobile computing system MeDNN, to facilitate extensive deployment of DNNs. They propose a Greed 2-D Partition (GTDP) which intelligently partitions the DNN model across distributed user devices according to the resources available to them. Next, they propose a compression method, Structured Model Compact Deployment (SMCD), which uses sparsity pruning to enhance the device-based inference process further. The implementation of MeDNN shows increasing the worker nodes from two to four helps greedy 2-D Partition to accelerate the DNN inference time by 1.86–2.44×. Moreover, the use of SMCD saves 26.5% of computing time and 14.2% of extra communication time all the while incurring minimal loss in accuracy.

c. **Model Early Exit**

A lot of classification tasks can be done accurately without executing the whole AI model (Zhou et al., 2019). The model early exit method uses the output of initial layers to obtain classification results, thereby speeding up the model inference process. This means we can complete the inference process using a DNN model partially. Hence, the classification task which can be inferred with confidence early, exits prematurely from one of the exit points present in different layers of the deep neural network. The inference process is completed within the Data samples, which can already be inferred with confidence, exit prematurely from one of the exit points present in different layers of the deep neural network (Shi et al., 2020). Hence, the main goal is to optimize the latency of the inference process. In this approach, each device runs the first layers of the AI model. If the device output does not meet the accuracy requirements, the remaining calculations are offloaded to the edge of the cloud.

d. **Edge Caching**

Edge Caching is implemented to reduce the overall latency of model inference. Prediction results of tasks are stored (cached) in edge servers (Xu et al., 2020) to promote reusability and reduce probing latency for AI applications. If the results demanded from the end device are not found in the edge server, the request is reverted to the cloud, where the whole model inference takes place. Drolia et al. (2017) proposed Cachier, which utilizes a caching model to accelerate the inference process of image-recognition applications. Cachier keeps the cached data in edge servers nearby to users by considering the spatiotemporal locality of requests. This approach helps to reduce the load of requests going to the cloud. Evaluating cachier on public datasets yielded 3 times acceleration in inference without hurting the accuracy. CNNCache (Xu et al., 2017), another caching mechanism which targets vision tasks, reuses the features extracted of similar image regions to speed up the inference process.

This caching mechanism uses two techniques; an image matching algorithm which recognizes similar image frames and CNN inference engine, which is cache-aware, that transmits the identified reusable regions through different layers and reutilizes the compute results in every layer. On average, this mechanism accelerates CNN model inference by 20.2% and even up to 47.1% under specific cases, with just a negligible loss in accuracy (up to 3.51%).

e. **Input Filtering**

The core idea behind input filtering is to remove non-essential data from the input and enhance inference. This helps to reduce the size of the incoming data, hence evading redundant computations, and as a result increasing the accuracy and energy efficiency and reducing the latency. NoScope (Kang et al., 2017), a system which leverages input filtering, reduces the cost of inference process by up to three times. NoScope implements a difference detector which helps to skip frames with little change or no target object by highlighting the temporal difference across frames.

f. **Model Selection**

At first, all the AI models are trained to perform the same task. Then, a model is adaptively selected for a specific task (considering the model's size, accuracy, and capabilities) during the online execution of an application. This technique optimizes accuracy, energy, and latency. For example, Park et al. (2015) also proposed a framework where the simple computations are executed using a smaller model, and only when the confidence of the small model is below a pre-set threshold will the inference be moved to a larger and more complex model. The goal is to use the small, energy-efficient model for computing the final inference results which significantly reduces energy consumption with minimal loss in accuracy. The results of this framework show a 53.7 and 94.1% reduction in energy consumption for ImageNet and MNSIT respectively with only 0.90% (ImageNet) and 0.12% (MNSIT) loss in accuracy. Another approach (Taylor et al., 2018) to implement model selection is to train a model offline to adaptively choose a DNN model based on a specific input and optimization constraint. This approach reduces the execution time by 1.8× and yields a 7.52% increase in inference accuracy when using the ImageNet Large Scale Visual Recognition Challenge 2012 dataset implemented on a Jetson TX2.

g. **Support for Multitenancy**

Typically, multiple applications run simultaneously on a single device, and without the support for multitenancy or heterogeneity of applications, the inference process will be inefficient (Zhou et al., 2019). Careful model selection for tasks and resource allocation in real time is required to achieve multitenancy. This will, in turn, reduce the memory footprint and energy cost. To this end, Mainstream (Jiang et al., 2018) leverages Knowledge Transfer learning to coordinate competing applications which utilize the same resource pool at the edge. Mainstream shares partial DNN compute among multiple applications which have been trained through transfer learning from the same "teacher" DNN model, thereby reducing total computation time per frame. Depending on the availability of certain resources and the applications running on an edge device/server, Mainstream dynamically decides during execution time, when to use the specialized DNNs to increase per frame accuracy and while utilizing the non-specialized base model to increase sharing and handle more frames per second.

h. **Application-specific optimization**
   Modifying the execution process of an application (Zhou et al., 2019) for increasing efficiency and reducing resource requirements is essential for model inference on the device to optimize memory footprint, energy efficiency, latency, and accuracy. However, these modifications can lead to a loss of inference accuracy. It is, therefore, necessary to settle a trade-off between resource cost and accuracy.

Table 3.2 shows correlation matrix which represents the positive and negative impacts an Enabling technology has on one or more of the key performance indicators for EI model inference.

## 3.6   COMPARATIVE ANALYSIS OF EI MODEL TRAINING AND INFERENCING AT EDGE

### Architectures

Edge servers are mainly used as relays for powerful cloud centers, undermining the true potential and benefits of edge intelligence. To this end, we need to bring the entire Lifecycle of AI to the edge, including both the training and inference processes. The execution of AI models is already edge-friendly since it does not require tremendous data and intensive computations compared to training. Hence, the four architectures of model inference, i.e., edge-based, device-based, edge-device, and edge-cloud, all utilize the edge server for the inference process. However, since training and building of a model requires enormous processing power, data from various IoT devices, and sophisticated hardware and software, the use of a central cloud is still prevalent. Except for the decentralized architecture, the centralized and hybrid architectures focus on offloading the exhaustive computations to the robust central servers. To match the advanced intelligent needs of IoT applications, the training and inference processes need to be implemented on the edge servers or end devices themselves.

### *Key Performance Indicators*

The KPIs for AI model training essentially evaluate the efficiency, cost, and privacy while training an AI algorithm. On the contrary, while executing the models, the main metric to be considered is the inference process's accuracy and speed. Even though some Key Performance Indicators, like latency, energy, privacy, and communication cost, appear in both model training and inference, their context is different in both processes. Latency refers to the delay caused by the transmission of input data and the computation-intensive tasks in the context of model training, while inference latency refers to the time it takes to run the model, including the pre-processing and post-processing stages. It generally depends on the resources available on the edge device. In the AI model training process, privacy protection can be achieved by offloading less privacy-sensitive data to an edge or cloud server. In the inference process, whether privacy protection is achieved is the way data is processed. The communication overhead during model inference greatly affects the quality of Service of EI applications. Since models are generally executed in a synergy of cloud, edge, and device, it is necessary to implement technologies such as model partitioning and model compression to enhance the performance of EI inference. In the training context, communication overhead refers to the transmission of data across various edge nodes, which causes latency and energy/bandwidth consumption, thus reducing the convergence speed of the AI model. Due to the energy constraints of end devices, both training and inference processes should be made energy-efficient, and hence energy cost is an essential metric for both processes. Memory footprint is the amount of main memory accessed by Central Processing Units (CPUs) and Graphics Processing Units (GPUs) during the resource-hungry inference process. Accuracy directly determines the correctness of output predicted by the AI model, i.e., the performance of the EI application.

## Enabling Technologies

Enabling technologies include frameworks, architectures, new algorithms, and technologies that help in improving the key performance indicators of model training and inference at the edge. Model training, which is a resource- and computation-intensive task, puts immense pressure on the central server, increasing the risk of privacy leakages and bandwidth consumption and latency. Therefore, to optimize the training process (by optimizing the KPIs) we need to distribute the training process among multiple devices and servers and bring the training process ultimately onto the device. Federated Learning, Gossip Training, and E-Tree, arguably the most talked-about approaches, help fulfill this very purpose. Gossip Training and E-Tree initiate the training process entirely in a distributed manner without dependence on a central cloud. On the other hand, Federated Learning requires a central authority to aggregate the local model updates to build the global model. Aggregation Frequency Control manages the frequency of these updates, thereby reducing the communication overhead and optimizing decentralized model training. Furthermore, Knowledge Transfer Learning is devised to decrease resource consumption, by reusing the training features and patterns learned from a base network. Model Compression and Model Splitting are two technologies common to EI model training and inference. In the context of model training, gradient compression is utilized to compress the local model updates. In contrast, AI models are compressed to work efficiently on resource-constrained end devices in model inference. Model Splitting or Partitioning is done during both the process (training and inference) by splitting the model between various devices or servers, thereby reducing latency and privacy leakages and optimizing energy consumption. Model Early Exit, Input Filtering, and Edge Caching are three technologies that help in reducing the latency of model inference. Early Exit leverages exit points present in different model layers, rendering the inference process efficient without executing the whole model. Input Filtering helps filter out the frames with non-target or redundant objects (especially in the field of Video-Analytics) to make the inference process faster. Edge Caching promotes the reusability of prediction results and training features from historical data sets by storing them in end devices and edge servers to reduce EI model inference's memory footprint and latency. Application-Specific optimization tremendously increases the accuracy of the inference process as the model execution is modified according to the specific application. This approach faces a lot of trade-offs that need to be handled carefully. Lastly, an EI model needs to run heterogeneous applications simultaneously, which will be impossible without the support for multitenancy, an essential technology for model inference at the edge.

## 3.7  Summary

This chapter covered all concepts of EdgeAI which will be required for its implementation in algorithmic government. We first introduced the concept of EdgeAI and explained the benefits of edge intelligence by highlighting the complementary relationship (AI for Edge and Edge for AI) between edge computing and artificial intelligence. We then described the various architectures of EdgeAI, ranging from a completely cloud-based architecture to an all-on-device architecture. We also talk about training and inference architectures specifically. Next, we elaborate on the various criteria used to evaluated model training and model inference at the edge, namely Latency, Communication, Privacy, Energy, Accuracy, and Memory Footprint. We then review existing frameworks and technologies, for EI model training and inference separately, which help to improve the efficacy of the two phases of AI model workflow by improving specific Key Performance Indicators. We also provided the impact of enabling technologies on each Key Performance Indicator for both the training and the inference process. Finally, we compared and analyzed various architectures, key metrics, and frameworks of EI model training and model inference to better understand the difference between the two processes.

## References

Blot, M., Picard, D., Cord, M., & Thome, N. (2016). *Gossip training for deep learning.* arXiv preprint arXiv: https://arxiv.org/abs/1611.09726

Calo, S. B., Touna, M., Verma, D. C., & Cullen, A. (2017, December). Edge computing architecture for applying AI to IoT. In *2017 IEEE International Conference on Big Data (Big Data)* (pp. 3012–3016). IEEE.

Chang, L., Zhang, Z., Li, P., Xi, S., Guo, W., Shen, Y., Xiong, Z., Kang, J., Niyato, D., Qiao, X., & Wu, Y. (2022). *6G-enabled Edge AI for Metaverse: Challenges, methods, and future research directions.* arXiv preprint arXiv: https://arxiv.org/abs/2204.06192

Drolia, U., Guo, K., Tan, J., Gandhi, R., & Narasimhan, P. (2017, June). Cachier: Edge-caching for recognition applications. In *2017 IEEE 37th International Conference on Distributed Computing Systems (ICDCS)* (pp. 276–286). IEEE.

Engstrom, D. F., Ho, D. E., Sharkey, C. M., & Cuéllar, M. F. (2020). *Government by algorithm: Artificial intelligence in federal administrative agencies* (NYU School of Law, Public Law Research Paper, pp. 20–54).

Gong, Y., Liu, L., Yang, M., & Bourdev, L. (2014). *Compressing deep convolutional networks using vector quantization.* arXiv preprint arXiv: https://arxiv.org/abs/1412.6115

Han, S., Pool, J., Tran, J., & Dally, W. J. (2015). *Learning both weights and connections for efficient neural networks.* arXiv preprint arXiv: https://arxiv.org/abs/1506.02626

Jiang, A. H., Wong, D. L. K., Canel, C., Tang, L., Misra, I., Kaminsky, M., Kozuch, M. A., Pillai, P., Andersen, D. G., & Ganger, G. R. (2018). Mainstream: Dynamic stem-sharing for multi-tenant video processing. In *2018 {USENIX} Annual Technical Conference ({USENIX}{ATC} 18)* (pp. 29–42).

Kang, D., Emmons, J., Abuzaid, F., Bailis, P., & Zaharia, M. (2017). *Noscope: Optimizing neural network queries over video at scale.* arXiv preprint arXiv: https://arxiv.org/abs/1703.02529

Lovén, L., Leppänen, T., Peltonen, E., Partala, J., Harjula, E., Porambage, P., Ylianttila, M., & Riekki, J. (2019). *EdgeAI: A vision for distributed, edge-native artificial intelligence in future 6G networks.* The 1st 6G Wireless Summit (pp. 1–2).

Mao, J., Yang, Z., Wen, W., Wu, C., Song, L., Nixon, K. W., Chen, X., Li, H., & Chen, Y. (2017, November). MeDNN: A distributed mobile system with enhanced partition and deployment for large-scale DNNs. In *2017 IEEE/ACM International Conference on Computer-Aided Design (ICCAD)* (pp. 751–756). IEEE.

McMahan, B., Moore, E., Ramage, D., Hampson, S., & Arcas, B. A. (2017, April). Communication-efficient learning of deep networks from decentralized data. In *Artificial Intelligence and Statistics* (pp. 1273–1282). PMLR.

Park, E., Kim, D., Kim, S., Kim, Y.-D., Kim, G., Yoon, S., & Yoo, S. (2015) Big/little deep neural network for ultra-low power inference. In *Proceedings of the 10th 2023 International Conference on Hardware/Software Codesign and System Synthesis* (pp. 124–132).

Sharma, R., Biookaghazadeh, S., Li, B., & Zhao, M. (2018, July). Are existing knowledge transfer techniques effective for deep learning with edge devices?

In *2018 IEEE International Conference on Edge Computing (EDGE)* (pp. 42–49). IEEE.

Shi, Y., Yang, K., Jiang, T., Zhang, J., & Letaief, K. B. (2020). Communication-efficient Edge AI: Algorithms and systems. *IEEE Communications Surveys & Tutorials, 22*(4), 2167–2191.

Taylor, B., Marco, V. S., Wolff, W., Elkhatib, Y., & Wang, Z. (2018). Adaptive deep learning model selection on embedded systems. *ACM SIGPLAN Notices, 53*(6), 31–43.

Wang, J., Zhang, J., Bao, W., Zhu, X., Cao, B., & Yu, P. S. (2018, July). Not just privacy: Improving performance of private deep learning in mobile cloud. In *Proceedings of the 24th ACM SIGKDD International Conference on Knowledge Discovery & Data Mining* (pp. 2407–2416).

Wang, S., Tuor, T., Salonidis, T., Leung, K. K., Makaya, C., He, T., & Chan, K. (2019). Adaptive federated learning in resource constrained edge computing systems. *IEEE Journal on Selected Areas in Communications, 37*(6), 1205–1221.

Xu, D., Li, T., Li, Y., Su, X., Tarkoma, S., Jiang, T., Crowcroft, J., & Hui, P. (2020). *Edge intelligence: Architectures, challenges, and applications.* arXiv preprint arXiv: https://arxiv.org/abs/2003.12172

Xu, M., Liu, X., Liu, Y., & Lin, F. (2017). *Accelerating convolutional neural networks for continuous mobile vision via cache reuse.*

Yang, L., Lu, Y., Cao, J., Huang, J., & Zhang, M. (2021). E-tree learning: A novel decentralized model learning framework for Edge AI. *IEEE Internet of Things Journal, 8,* 11290–11304.

Ye, Y., Li, S., Liu, F., Tang, Y., & Hu, W. (2020). EdgeFed: Optimized federated learning based on edge computing. *IEEE Access, 8,* 209191–209198.

Zhou, Z., Chen, X., Li, E., Zeng, L., Luo, K., & Zhang, J. (2019). Edge intelligence: Paving the last mile of artificial intelligence with edge computing. *Proceedings of the IEEE, 107*(8), 1738–1762.

# CHAPTER 4

# EdgeAI Use Cases for Algorithmic Government

**Abstract** In this chapter we review some use cases of EdgeAI for algorithmic government. Some of the use cases include Facial Recognition for Suspects at Public Places, Social Network Analysis (SNA) for analyzing citizen behavior, Voice enabled AI-based personal assistants, and Industrial safety through cameras and sensors. We propose different architectures and enabling technologies for each use case, aimed at optimizing the various key performance indicators of model training and inference in those particular scenarios.

**Keywords** EdgeAI · Architectures · Key Performance Indicators · Facial Recognition · Social Network Analysis · AI-based personal assistants · Border security

## 4.1 Facial Recognition for Suspects at Public Places

In crowded, cramped, and chaotic airport environments, face recognition technology is deployed to catch criminals or illegal immigrants. Figure 4.1 gives an overview of Facial Recognition for Suspects at Public Places. For example, the US Customs and Border Protection (CBP) required airports to buy cameras for facial recognition. The system works

© The Author(s), under exclusive license to Springer Nature Singapore Pte Ltd. 2023
R. Gupta et al., *EdgeAI for Algorithmic Government*,
https://doi.org/10.1007/978-981-19-9798-3_4

by detecting a face or multiple faces in a static or video setting and matching it with an identity by running it across a database of known faces. CBP's primary vendor of facial recognition software, Unisys, utilizes deep learning models for processing images to estimate a person's age. The training set for a model like this will contain the known faces of all the people residing in a specific geographic location (district, city, or country), which can be accessible by the airports, famous tourist destinations, market places, and other busy places of that area. The model should thus be trained in a centralized architecture, as the cloud provides a single homogeneous environment for the entire training process. The analysis of the faces captured by the camera has to be very quick since the sensors have to record the footage to detect any viable suspects continuously.

Therefore, reducing latency is crucial, and the inference must occur in a device-based mode or an edge-device mode. Model compression can be implemented to reduce the model size with minimal loss in accuracy, hence decreasing latency and the memory footprint of the software. Suppose the inference occurs in an edge-device mode. In that case, the model can be partitioned between the device and the edge server/servers, further attenuating the pressure from resource-constrained terminal devices in play. We also propose input filtering to help discard the redundant and unnecessary frames, to speed up the inference process and also enhance the accuracy of the computations.

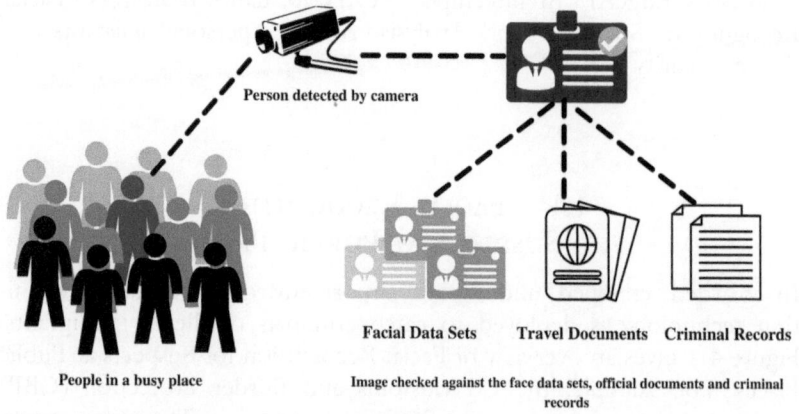

Fig. 4.1 Facial recognition process for suspects at airports, markets, and busy public places

## 4.2    Social Network Analysis (SNA)
## for Analyzing Citizen Behavior

Nowadays, the Internet is an inseparable part of everyone's life. People spend hours on social media, e-commerce, writing political views or reviews about their purchased products, watching their favourite shows and movies, and much more. Figure 4.2 shows how social network analysis is used for analyzing user behavior/intent. Analysis of users' behavior over social media helps a lot of applications cater to the unique needs of people. SNA is already being used to detect psychological diseases, establish employee networks in a company for guiding HR activities, LSDM events to group people with similar interests, assess customer satisfaction, and more. For example, Natural Language Processing tools can analyze users' sentiments, opinions, and interests. A clustering model can be leveraged to identify people with similar interests. Hybrid architecture for training can be utilized in this scenario, where the local training model updates from each user's device are aggravated to obtain a global model. The clustering model can then be trained in a central cloud utilizing the data from various user devices.

Federated Learning can help facilitate the training process, thereby reducing latency and privacy risks. The frequency of controlling the local model updates is essential, and hence Aggregation Frequency Control should be implemented to optimize the approach of FL. The inference process of the model can take place in a device-based manner, where the analysis results in the form of recommendations or feedback can be provided to the user then and there. The user's behavior is tracked over various applications; hence the support for multitenancy is essential for the

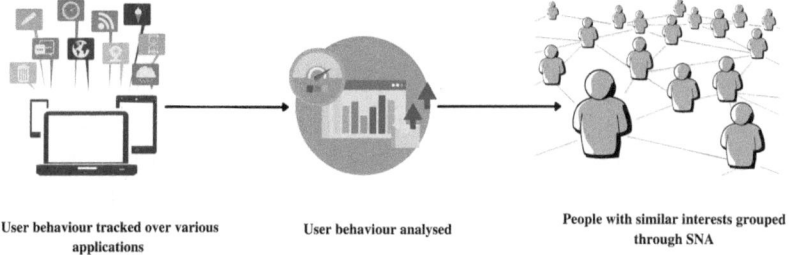

User behaviour tracked over various     User behaviour analysed     People with similar interests grouped
applications                                                         through SNA

**Fig. 4.2**   Social network analysis for analyzing user behavior/intent

model to execute efficiently. Application-Specific optimization approaches are also recommended to control the resources being used by each application, thereby leading to a decrease in latency and memory footprint, and an increase in the accuracy of the analysis done by the model.

## 4.3    AI in Healthcare

AI can diagnose diseases and go through medical records and large caseloads at a rate much higher than humans. In one case study, deep learning algorithms beat 11 pathologists at detecting breast cancer. Other than diagnostic processes, it is also used in medicine development, treatment protocol development, personalized medicine, and patient monitoring. Furthermore, AI software is needed to organize operations to implement cost-effectiveness, decrease staff load, and increase customer satisfaction by optimizing various resources. Hybrid architecture can be utilized so that a central cloud can take care of the resource-intensive computations required for the different AI algorithms used in healthcare. Here, preserving privacy is essential since we are dealing with sensitive medical records of patients. Hence, federated learning and model splitting can be implemented to curb privacy leakages. Inference can take play either in a device-based, edge-based, or edge-cloud manner depending on the intensity of the algorithms and the emergency of the task. For example, diagnostic processes and patient monitoring can occur in a device-based mode while analyzing medical history and other records can be inferred in the cloud. Privacy, energy, latency, and accuracy are things that need to be taken care of. To this end, we propose Model Selection to ensure the accuracy of results. Moreover, Model Compression and the partition should also be implemented to reduce the latency, energy cost, and privacy risks.

## 4.4    Voice Enabled AI-Based Personal Assistants

AI assistants like Siri, Alexa, and Cortana have raised the standard of living even further. Without even lifting a finger, people can make calls, send texts, play music, and do much more with the help of these intelligent agents. Government agents can turn to these Robo-assistants for performing redundant and easy tasks such as managing or resetting passwords, scheduling meetings, requesting information about various kinds of things such as important upcoming events, or even searching for information in lengthy reports. Public services can also be enhanced through intelligent voice agents as they can provide a 24*7 automated help desk for citizens, help fill out basic forms or fetch publicly available information. Apple's Siri utilizes a mixture of Deep Neural Network (DNN) models and Gaussian Mixture Models (GMM) for performing speech synthesis, i.e. the artificial production of human speech. The training samples include hours of human speech recorded at 48 kHz. The text processing from the speech is used to analyze the content and take further action. The features such as making calls, sending texts, etc., are implemented after analyzing the tone, pitch, modulation detected in the voice. Figure 4.3 depicts how speech is analyzed by AI to execute the user's request. The text is then processed to infer the meaning of the request or query. A centralized training architecture can be used to train this model. Since some of the basic features of voice-enabled assistants will be the same for everyone, transfer learning can be used to train a base network, and the functionalities acquired from it can be used to train a student network on a target data set. The inference process should take place on the device itself, giving real-time responses to personalized queries and requests from officials and citizens. Reducing latency and memory footprint is essential; hence model compression can be implemented to optimize the inference process further.

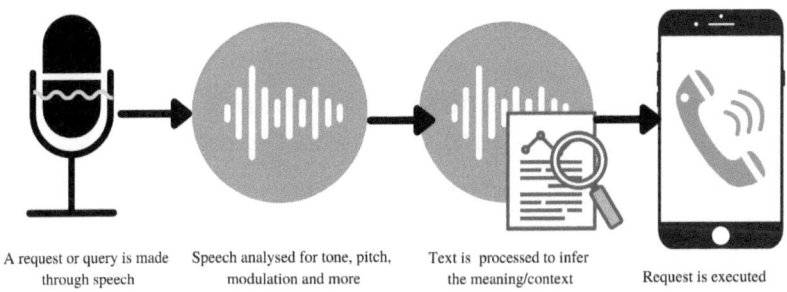

A request or query is made through speech    Speech analysed for tone, pitch, modulation and more    Text is processed to infer the meaning/context    Request is executed

**Fig. 4.3**  Voice enabled AI-based personal assistants

## 4.5    INDUSTRIAL SAFETY
### THROUGH CAMERAS AND SENSORS

Hazardous situations frequently arise in manufacturing, coal, mining, and mineral industries, leading to fatal accidents. AI technology can help reduce accidents, especially in heavy machinery and large assembly lines, by predicting the faults in safety measurements and equipment. Real-time footage can be analyzed thoroughly and faster than is humanly possible. Cameras and sensors can monitor the performance of people in a factory. Timely guidance can be provided if people don't comply with the regulations, sending warnings to the managers, curbing improper practices, and improving industrial safety. Sensors can also be placed on forklifts and other equipment to communicate with each other to avoid collisions or dropping heavy objects inside the plant.

A decentralized architecture would be best suited for training the AI model, where many devices collaborate to obtain the global model. Gossip training can be utilized to ensure complete independence from a central server. Device-based or edge-device-based inference can be implemented to execute the model on the nearby edge devices. Reducing energy costs is vital since the edge devices are resource-constrained. Moreover, accidents can present a life-or-death situation; latency should also be minimal. To this end, we propose model compression and partition to ease the load on the resource constricted edge devices and input filtering for efficiently and accurately selecting only the relevant frames from the continuous real-time footage of the plant.

## 4.6    EDGEAI FOR BORDER
### SECURITY AND MILITARY PLANNING

In border security, face recognition technology is widely used to detect threats at travel ports. Sensors can also be used in custom processes to spot the migration of illegal things or people, thereby stopping crimes like smuggling. In the military, environment data and historic mission data can be used along with drones and satellite images to survey or detect any unknown objects on the field. Moreover, predictive analysis on this data can help to understand future mission scenarios better and allocate resources cost-effectively by collaborating between different missions. Figure 4.4 shows how industrial safety is implemented by using concepts

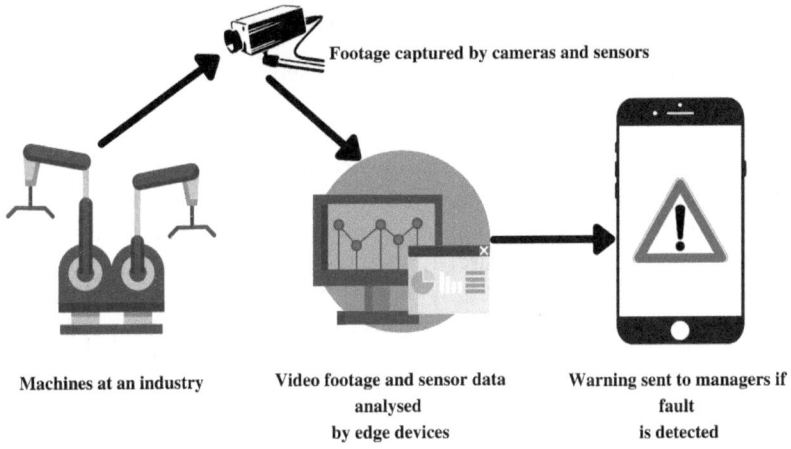

Footage captured by cameras and sensors

Machines at an industry | Video footage and sensor data analysed by edge devices | Warning sent to managers if fault is detected

**Fig. 4.4** Industrial safety through cameras and sensors

of EdgeAI. Computer vision technology can also be used to detect faulty equipment and algorithms can be used to plan maintenance schedules.

Since many edge devices are at play here, a decentralized architecture would pose perfectly for security and military planning. Privacy preservation is the number one priority; hence, we need to use enabling technologies that reduce privacy risks during model training and inference. Federated learning and gossip training enable a model in a decentralized manner while preserving privacy since algorithms are trained on distributed edge devices without having to exchange the data between them. Model splitting is another approach to preserve privacy where a model is split into two parts, both of which are kept in a separate location. We propose the device-based mode or the edge-device mode architecture for the model inference. Model compression and partition help reduce latency, privacy risks, and enable efficient execution of the complex AI models in resource-constrained edge devices. Since a lot of monitoring and detecting is involved in security, Input Filtering and Model Early Exit can be implemented, where data samples that can be inferred with confidence pre-maturely exit from one of the exit points without executing the entire model. This also has a positive impact on latency and privacy.

## 4.7    IDENTIFYING CITIZENS WHO CAN BE VICTIMIZED

Combining emotion detection with facial detection can be very useful for identifying people in danger or dangerous people. Facial emotion recognition analyzes people's feelings and emotions from static images or video sources. The analysis process occurs in three steps—face recognition, expression recognition, classifying sentiment according to the detected expression. Expressions are identified by looking at features such as eyebrows, lips, etc. Figure 4.5 shows how emotion recognition is deployed at the edge to identify victims at public places. For example, raised eyebrows, wide-opened eyes, and jaw clenched or dropped could indicate that a person is in fear. Cameras placed all over the city continuously analyze the footage it receives to check for people who can be victimized. Once a person has been identified to be in danger, alerts are sent to the nearby police stations or other authorities in charge. In this way, a lot of crimes can be prevented as instant help is provided.

Since training the model includes a lot of data ets for facial emotion recognition, the cloud architecture offers a homogenous environment for this process. A device-based or an edge-device inference is needed for detecting the victims as quickly as possible since it can be a matter of life and death. Model compression and model early exit can further decrease the latency and energy cost. Inference accuracy of the model can be enhanced with input filtering.

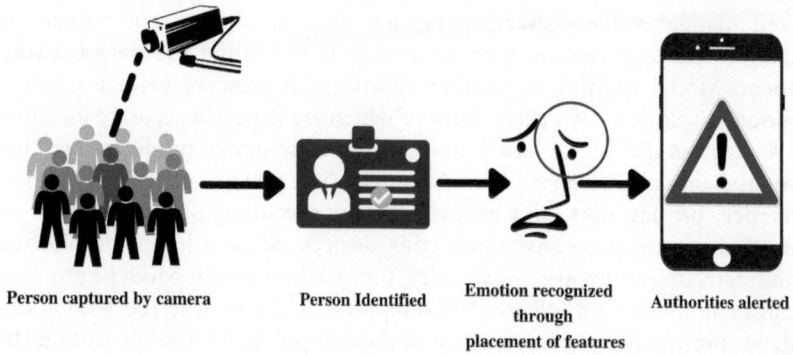

Person captured by camera    Person Identified    Emotion recognized through placement of features    Authorities alerted

**Fig. 4.5** Identifying citizens who can be victimized and providing instant help for public safety

## 4.8    SUMMARY

This chapter reviews use cases of algorithmic government and how EdgeAI can be integrated with them to enable federal agencies to function more efficiently. The cases reviewed are facial recognition at busy places, Social Network Analysis for analyzing citizen behavior, AI in healthcare, voice-enabled personal assistants, industrial safety through cameras and sensors, AI in border security and military planning and lastly, identifying citizens who can be victimized. Keeping in mind the goal and critical evaluation metrics for each use case, we proposed suitable EI model training and inference architectures and enabling technologies. This is generalized in the next chapter as a framework.

CHAPTER 5

# Implications and Future Scope

**Abstract** We begin this chapter by proposing a conceptual framework which helps to determine whether it is feasible and beneficial to adopt EdgeAI in a particular application of Algorithmic Government. Next, we discuss challenges in edge computing which include Network Integration and Resource Management, Cloud and Edge Coexistence and Reliability of Edge Devices. Further, we talk about ethical issues in AI and EdgeAI specifically, and several policies and guidelines which aim at addressing these problems. Finally, we discuss technological implications of adopting EdgeAI followed by emerging hardware devices which facilitate EdgeAI applications.

**Keywords** Technological implications · Ethical issues · Hardware · Accelerators · Field Programmable Gate Arrays · GPUs

## 5.1 Conceptual Framework

Based on the concepts covered around Edge Computing, EdgeAI and their applications for large-scale decision-making in Algorithmic Government, a conceptual framework for decision-making to adopt EdgeAI has been derived, as shown in Fig. 5.1.

© The Author(s), under exclusive license to Springer Nature       67
Singapore Pte Ltd. 2023
R. Gupta et al., *EdgeAI for Algorithmic Government*,
https://doi.org/10.1007/978-981-19-9798-3_5

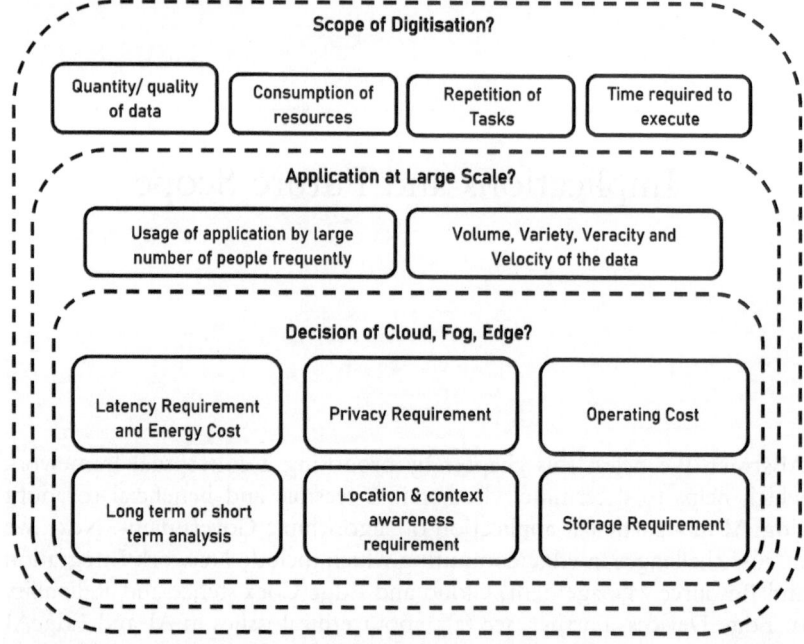

**Fig. 5.1** Conceptual framework for decision-making on adoption of EdgeAI for Algorithmic Government applications

The outermost layer questions the scope of digitization for the Algorithmic Government application. It is important that if digital assets are prominently attached with the application, then only it is valuable to get into the depth of EdgeAI architectural implementation. So quality of data (physical/digital, numeric/text/multimedia), rate of consumption of different resources and data, repeatability in the various tasks to consume the data, and time to execute the applications are some of the major concerns addressed while answering whether an application can be digitized or not. Once we understand these aspects, for example in social network analysis for citizens there was a huge scope of digitization possible, then we move on to the next layer.

The next important dimension that comes into consideration is whether that digital application has scope of large-scale decision-making or not. For smaller applications, data assets would not be that large that we may have to consider different network and storage structures. Hence, usage by mass number of people and big data characteristics answers that whether decision-making is impacted at large scale or not. This impacts different KPIs like latency, speed, cost, and impact.

And the third layer considered for decision is toward the choice of Cloud, Fog, or Edge Computing choice. It may not be necessary that Edge is the best solution in all scenarios. Hence we have to consider choices around latency requirement, energy cost, privacy requirement, operating cost, length of analysis (short term or long term), location and context awareness, and the storage requirement. We have defined different requirements for cloud, fog, and edge in preceding chapters and that helps us in understanding whether Edge is a good choice for us. And if it is a good choice, then we move to adopting EdgeAI with different approaches and technologies for model training & inferencing (as covered in Chapter 3).

## 5.2  Challenges in Edge Computing: Network Integration and Resource Management

In EdgeAI, resource-exhaustive AI-based applications run in a decentralized edge computing environment. The network edge comprises devices ranging from static sensors, cameras, and laptops to moving vehicles and mobile phones. Advanced network designs with computation awareness are needed to share the data among various edge devices efficiently. Hence, wired, wireless, and cellular network technologies should easily blend (Rimal et al., 2017) and coordinate together to provide edge computing devices. Furthermore, self-governing network infrastructures are needed to efficiently implement the EI services and allow the new edge nodes to configure themselves automatically (Zhou et al., 2019). Vice-versa, edge devices should also support the multitude of network architectures and features to implement AI technologies seamlessly and efficiently (Rimal et al., 2017). The correct distribution of limited network resources to various edge devices deployed at the edge is essential in large-scale dynamic EI applications like smart cities where sudden, unpredictable situations may arise and orchestrate resources among edge devices. Designing such networks becomes complicated as limited bandwidth, storage, etc., are shared among various devices and servers according to their dynamic needs. This calls for a resource management scheme which is not required for conventional networks.

## 5.3    CHALLENGES IN EDGE COMPUTING: CLOUD AND EDGE COEXISTENCE

We know that edge devices and servers complement the cloud, and they all work together for the effective execution of AI applications. Deciding whether an application should be executed at the centralized cloud or the edge is difficult since it depends on the available resources present at the various infrastructures and the application's requirements (Rimal et al., 2017). The problem arises in figuring out which portion of the application should be offloaded to the cloud, or a nearby edge server, making the design of underlying architectures of edge computing devices complex (Rimal et al., 2017). Moreover, the coexistence of edge and cloud must be planned, considering the limited available network resources. Collaboration of the devices and various servers to optimize computations, communication, and storage allocations are uncompromisable. Since different organizations generally own edge devices, servers, cloudlets, and cloud, interoperability issues may also arise. A common platform to manage multiple cloudlets, clouds, and edge devices is required to enhance network performance and reduce costs.

## 5.4    CHALLENGES IN EDGE COMPUTING: RELIABILITY OF EDGE DEVICES

As discussed in the previous section, the inference process of almost all use cases is happening on the device itself. In sensitive and grave situations such as industrial safety, border security, and healthcare, the devices have to meet a threshold of reliability and endurance which poses a challenge for the design of devices (Rimal et al., 2017). Furthermore, a user's mobility should also be taken into account. Mobile Edge Computing (MEC) must provide seamless continuity of service and mobility of Virtual Machines (VM) despite the location of the user. Since the mobility of VMs responds to several factors, like processing speed, volume of data, compression ratio, and bandwidth, making it challenging to perform such VM migration smoothly without compromising the quality of the experience. Since many uncertain and time-varying circumstances must be well predicted, artificial intelligence algorithms must store a lot of historical data for accurate predictions (Rimal et al., 2017). However, caching resources are limited and used primarily for caching popular content; hence, there is a trade-off between predictive accuracy and content caching. Moreover, various edge nodes may be providing different EI functionalities; hence, it is essential to design a platform that can help users promptly identify the appropriate EI service providers according to their requirements.

## 5.5   Ethical Issues in EdgeAI

The increasing use of AI in government is underpinned by its ability to personalize public services, reduce operational costs, and improve decision-making by analyzing the wealth of data generated by millions of IoT devices. According to Deloitte (William et al., 2017), the automation of government tasks has the potential to save 1.2 billion working hours as well as $41.1 billion in operational costs. Realizing these benefits, governments all across the globe have increasingly incorporated AI technologies in various fields. Apart from the use cases we have reviewed in previous sections, we can also find AI being utilized in Australia, in the form of chatbots assisting the Taxation Office and the Department of Human Services. In the United States, a system to dynamic real-time traffic signal control called Scalable Urban Traffic Control (SURTRAC) has been devised to manage traffic flows on urban road networks (Smith et al., 2013). As a result of implementation on the Pittsburgh 9-intersection road network, travel time and vehicle emissions have been significantly reduced compared to existing signal controls.

The adoption of AI has especially skyrocketed during the outbreak of Covid-19. The use of drones for crowd surveillance has become especially prevalent. Cyient, an Indian multinational technological company, aided the Telangana police with aerial surveillance during lockdown to manage unpredictable situations. Autonomous Vehicles were leveraged in China to conduct deliveries from Beijing to the Guanggu Field Hospital, mitigating the pressure on healthcare workers and preventing their exposure to the virus. Surveillance company BlueDot developed an AI model to track the spread of SARSCoV2 and predicted its outbreak long before epidemiologists. It is thus evident that Artificial Intelligence and Machine Learning paradigms have become ubiquitous.

It is therefore necessary to ensure that these self-learning technologies comply with specific social and political guidelines, keeping in mind the ethical principles that ensure human safety. If not controlled carefully, AI will embrace the good parts of humanity along with the bad. Biases in algorithms, exposure of privacy sensitive user data, and automating important decisions which can gravely impact the society, are some of the ethical concerns being faced by all the stakeholders involved with these intelligent systems. The dark side of AI can exacerbate the extant problems of marginalization of underprivileged communities, racism, gender inequality, and much more.

Biases can be fed in the form of input data either unconsciously or consciously by the program developers. If a dataset has more white faces, it can lead to the algorithm identifying the non-white faces as inanimate objects. For instance, in the UK, an immigration algorithm for processing visa applications (August 2020) seemed to prefer "people from rich white countries" over people of color who were pushed to the back of the line. In a similar case, Correctional Offender Management Profiling for Alternative Sanctions (Compas), a program used for risk assessment in a US court was twice as likely to flag black defendants as potentially recidivists than white individuals. Algorithms can also mimic gender stereotypes as has been seen in the case of Google News articles. Word embedding systems may associate *female* with *receptionist* and *male* with *athlete*. Such prejudices exhibited by machines can unfairly disadvantage the communities of certain people and gravely affect their lives.

Privacy violation is also one of the major concerns regarding the use of AI. The FBI's National Security Agency's (NSA) mass surveillance program is one such case which has known to infringe the rights of American citizens by wrongly sifting through their personal messages and emails. The NSA's mass surveillance program is monitored by a set of government agencies that allow governments to exfiltrate communications in transit over the Internet and receive communications directly from at least eight major tech companies without a warrant. This program was an extension of the Foreign Intelligence Surveillance Act that allowed the FBI to intercept communications of terrorist organizations and other foreign government agents provided they could present legal justifications to the FISA court. This surveillance can scan all communications matching certain search terms and patterns, and can generate large amounts of inadvertently collected information, including communications from US citizens, which can be searched by government agencies afterwards. Therefore, we can see that the positives of AI can easily be mitigated by its malicious exploitation.

In the case of EdgeAI specifically, where applications are processed at the network edge, certain characteristics of edge can raise additional ethical concerns. Unlike the cloud, edge is a confederation of numerous stakeholders (service providers and users). The service providers can further include platform providers, software providers, organizations that own the edge nodes (Servers) and end user devices which provide the data. In the edge environment, a user can either be a data provider or a consumer. Therefore, specific models or guidelines are needed to effectively accelerate the integration of diverse stakeholders by defining social, political, and ethical boundaries (Varghese et al., 2016) for the use or ownership of edge nodes. For example, in the case of facial recognition at busy places, a clear mechanism is required to decide which devices are allowed to sense and provide the data for analysis while complying with the ethical guidelines.

Autonomous vehicles use a decentralized architecture to sense and process real-time data from various edge nodes for analyzing traffic flows, vehicle or pedestrian detection, location awareness, and more. Everyone makes ethical decisions on a daily basis. When drivers choose to apply the brakes to avoid hitting a pedestrian, they are making an ethical decision to transfer the risk from the pedestrian to the occupants of the vehicle. A situation may also arise where a car with broken brakes is heading toward a grandmother and a child, and deviating a little can save one of them. In the case of an AV, it is an algorithm facing these ethical dilemmas. If human life is at stake, will the program developers be held accountable or the EI service providers?

A similar case can be made for EdgeAI in healthcare. Several policies and guidelines have already been formulated for developing AI technologies which can provide solutions to a lot of the aforementioned ethical challenges. Committees of The IEEE Global Initiative on Ethics of Autonomous and Intelligent Systems, ("The IEEE Global Initiative") designed the Ethical Aligned Design to engender discussions on how to incorporate social and ethical considerations while designing intelligent systems. The document talks about three metrics to be kept in mind while developing these technologies; Human rights, well-being (of citizens) and accountability. Potential legal frameworks dictating the accountability of stakeholders or subjecting the intelligent systems to property law are also mentioned in the document. Various government organizations as well as software companies have also come up with their own guidelines like the UK Guidance on the AI auditing framework, EU Ethics guidelines for trustworthy AI, Singapore Model AI Governance Framework, AI at Google: our principles, Microsoft AI Principals and IBM Trusted AI for Business. While these frameworks dictate the implementation of social and ethical consideration in developing AI technologies, building ethical codes for the integration of intelligent machines with the edge architecture is essential.

## 5.6   TECHNOLOGICAL IMPLICATIONS

With advancements in technology, Artificial Intelligence has permeated our personal lives and the fields of economy, socio-culture, and politics. The integration of Artificial Intelligence into decision-making for public services is changing how governments operate worldwide. Algorithms help the government in various ways, including virtual assistants for busy civil servants, automated public services, and algorithmic decision-making processes. In such cases, the implementation of algorithms will occur on a massive scale and possibly affect the lives of entire communities. The cloud-centric architecture of Artificial Intelligence brings out challenges of latency, overhead communication, and significant privacy risks. Owing to the huge amount of data produced by IoT devices, the data analysis must be performed at the forefront of the network. As more and more government agencies are automated, there is a strict requirement that AI models be trained and inferred quickly, accurately, and resource-efficiently. This introduces the need for edge computing in algorithmic government. To this end, we proposed EdgeAI (the confluence of edge computing and AI), which implements AI at the network edge. The implications of EdgeAI include scalable solutions for large-scale government applications, improved speed and service times, and a better privacy preserving architecture.

A. **Scalability and Interoperability**: Government services such as smart cities, smart healthcare, and decision-making leveraging social network analysis occur on a very large scale and hence require scalable deployment of AI applications. In a cloud architecture, where the entire load is on a central server, managing a huge network of billions of IoT devices is not easy. Simultaneous processing of the data produced by user devices is tedious. Also, the problem is exacerbated if additional nodes need to be added to the network. Large-scale extensions can not only slow down the system, but also cause system failures. To combat these challenges, edge provides a decentralized architecture which allows the addition of new servers and devices without affecting other components of the network.

The localized training and inference of applications on user devices help to perform operations with the same ease for a single user or for, let's say, a million users. Smart cities are complex systems made up of computing technologies, big data analytics, and IoT devices with the goal to provide services like smart healthcare, smart traffic control, smart streetlights, smart education, smart waste management, and much more. This requires an efficient utilization of the resources to lead to a better standard of life for citizens. However, reaching this goal requires a high degree of support for developing and running applications in complex, dynamic environments. In such a case edge not only provides a scalable solution owing to the expansive nature of smart cities and meeting the ever-increasing demands of citizens, but also builds a network for the interoperability of heterogeneous devices.

B. **Speed and Reliability**: Applications that are time-sensitive and require context awareness such as detecting a heart attack, managing real-time traffic flow, facial recognition at airports, industrial safety, and military planning call for very fast data sourcing and analysis. It is only by understanding how crowded the roads are at any given time that it is possible to know whether to close a particular road or change the mode of traffic lights to avoid traffic jams. Relying on a cloud-centric architecture would mean that data from various heterogeneous sources (vehicles, cameras on streets, vehicle sensors) would first be transmitted to the cloud for analysis. The latency introduced can lead to the data required being outdated. This can result in congestion of roads or even grave situations like accidents. In addition to this, applications running on the edge can operate independently in places with unreliable network such as in fields where military works may deploy drones, or for safety purposes in offshore industries. EdgeAI thus provides a reliable and opportunistic environment for speedy interoperability of end user devices and quick execution of AI models even in inconstant network environments leading to a better Quality of Experience of edge applications.

C. **Security and Data Sovereignty**: Public services and government operations deal with a lot of confidential information which if not processed carefully can lead to grave repercussions. In the cloud architecture, the data has to traverse from terminal devices to the central cloud for processing and analysis purposes. Storing, analyzing, and processing privacy sensitive data in a different location poses severe threats to security. Shared resources on the same physical machine can lead to unwanted secondary channels between malicious and real resources. Searching through official government documents, digitized filling of important forms (passports and visas) or the real-time analysis of the footage collected by drones for border security are some use cases of algorithmic government which require a highly efficient privacy preserving framework for their deployment. Implementing AI at the edge rather than the cloud or fog allows for the data to be processed locally, making it less susceptible to any privacy risks. Malicious attackers to the cloud or Denial-of-Service attacks in the fog can lead to malfunctioning of the entire network. However, if a single edge device is compromised, that device can either be dealt with independently or disconnected from the network, leading to an overall secure network. Moreover, movement of data across national and regional borders can cause violation of certain data security laws. EdgeAI provides a local environment for the deployment of AI models which helps to process data close to its source and within the confines of applicable data sovereignty laws, such as the European Union's General Data Protection Regulation (GDPR) or California's California Consumer Privacy Act (CCPA). The local processing of data also helps in obfuscating or securing any sensitive data before it is sent to the cloud or primary data centers in other jurisdictions.

## 5.7    EMERGING HARDWARE AND FRAMEWORKS FOR EDGEAI SPECIFIC APPLICATIONS

Most Edge devices are resource-constrained and battery-limited, making them unenviable to realize the concept of Edge Intelligence, which pushes storage and compute power closer to the user devices/points of data sources. This has propelled the need for Edge specific frameworks such as TensorFlow Lite and Caffe2, hardware such as CPUs, GPUs, FGPAs, and ASICs, and edge devices such as Raspberry Pi 3B, Jetson Tx2, and Jetson Nano. Zou et al. (2019), reviews several state-of-the-art ML processors against the specialized tasks they are meant to perform and their power/energy efficiency. Moreover, several model architecture-circuits co-design for facilitating EI applications have been emerging in the industry as well as the academia.

A general-purpose Hardware and Software Co-Design Framework aimed at achieving Energy-Efficient Edge AI proposed by Jayakodi et al. (2021) performs inference adaptive to specific inputs on a DNN of commensurate complexity. Furthermore, it deploys this chosen DNN on an edge platform using a resource management policy. Their experiments on mobile devices demonstrate efficacy of energy utilization with negligible loss in accuracy. Wan et al. (2021) present NeuRRAM, a multi-modal edge AI chip using Resistive random-access memory (RRAM)-based compute-in-memory (CIM) architectures to achieve unprecedented energy efficiency across diverse AI workloads, hence promising efficiency, versatility as well as accuracy. It guarantees $5\times$-$8\times$ better energy efficiency than previous techniques implemented over various computational bit-precisions, a versatile reconfigurable chip for various model architectures and a 99% inference accuracy on MNIST, 85.7% on CIFAR-10 image classification, 84.7% accuracy on Google speech command recognition, and a 70% reduction in image reconstruction error on a Bayesian image recovery task. In this section, we will focus on Edge devices and related hardware.

### *AI Accelerators, Field Programmable Gate Arrays, and Devices*

Most of the energy required by AI inference is used to fetch parameters and weights from the primary memory to the Processing Elements (PE) where the computations are actually performed. Fetching from the primary memory increases latency and requires a considerable amount of energy. This drives the need for acceleration units at the edge which helps in providing near instant results for interactive EI applications. Table 5.1 summarizes the specifications of Hardware devices mentioned in this section. AI accelerators are special purpose processors which assist the traditional processing units by facilitating very fast vector and tensor computations and are optimized to handle AI workloads. The Intel Movidius Myriad X VPU is a dedicated hardware accelerator for on-device DNN inference and Computer Vision applications. It supports Caffe and TensorFlow models [intel].

**Table 5.1**  Hardware specifications for various devices used for EdgeAI implementation

| Device | CPU/GPU | Memory | Type |
|---|---|---|---|
| The Intel Movidius Myriad X | 16-core CPU 700 MHz | 2.5 MB | SoC |
| Google Edge TPU | 4-core Ctx.A53 & Ctx.-M4 @1.5 GHz Vivante GC7000 (32 GFLOPs) | 1 GB LPDDR4 | SoC/USB |
| M1076 Mythic AMP | – | – | SoC |
| Syntiant NDP | – | – | SoC |
| Jetson Nano | 4-core CPU, GPU | 4 GB | SOM |
| Jetson TX2 NX | 6-core CPUs, GPU | 4 GB | SOM |
| Jetson Xavier NX | 6-core CPU, GPU | 8 GB | PCIe |
| Jetson AGX Xavier | 8-core CPU, GPU | 32 GB | SOM |
| OpenMV Cam H7 R2 | STM32H743VI ARM Cortex M7 processor running at 480 MHz | 1 MB SRAM and 2 MB of flash | USB |
| Syntiant Tiny Machine Learning dev board | CPU 48 MHz | 32 kB | SBC |
| Raspberry Pi 4 | 4-core CPU 1.5 GHz | 8 GB | SBC |
| Raspberry Pi Pico | Dual-core Arm Cortex-M0 + processor, flexible clock running up to 133 MHZ | 264kB on-chip SRAM | Microcontroller development board |

Google Edge TPU, used to deploy TensorFlow Lite models is an application-specific integrated circuit which allows users to run benchmark AI model architectures such as Inception-ResNetV2, MobileNet v2, and DeepLap V3, among others in a power efficient manner [coral]. The M1076 Mythic AMP provides the computing power of a desktop GPU while consuming just $1/10^{th}$ the power. It also provides storage of up to 80 M weight parameters and on-chip DNN model inference without any external memory. The M1076 supports standard frameworks such as Pytorch, Caffe, and TensorFlow. The Syntiant NDP series provides low-power AI solutions (vision, sensor, and speech) for battery-powered systems and supports always-on person presence detection use cases.

Field Programming Gate Arrays are also being widely used for the executing of AI at the edge. They are semiconductor devices which can be programmed and reprogrammed to build processors for ML specific tasks. Intel offers a variety of edge-centric FGPAs such as the Intel MAX series for low-power and small-form factor applications, Cyclone 10 LP FGPA and Cyclone 1 V FGPA for balanced power and performance, and Cyclone 10 GX FGPA and Cyclone V FGPA for applications requiring enhanced bandwidth. The flexibility of FGPAs allows them to build AI accelerators as well. NVDLA by Nvidia (Wang et al., 2019) and Navion (Suleiman et al., 2019) are examples of accelerators which have been implemented in hardware using FGPAs. NVDIA has also launched a variety Edge GPUs commonly used for performing vector calculations in Machine Learning. These GPUs include the Jetson Nano, Jetson TX2 NX, Jetson Xavier NX, and Jetson AGX Xavier.

OpenMV Cam H7 R2 is a microcontrollable board with a removable camera module system which can be programmed in python. It offers a full speed USB interface to a computer and an MT9M114 image sensor is capable of taking $640 \times 480$ 8-bit Grayscale images or $640 \times 480$ 8-bit BAYER images at 40 FPS when the resolution is above $320 \times 240$ and 80 FPS when it is below. OpenMV Cam can be used to run TensorFlow Lite models, for frame differencing, color tracing, face detection, and more. The Syntiant's Tiny MachineLearning Board is embedded with the Syntiant NDP101 Neural Decision Processor, and onboard microphone and BMI160 sensor making it ideal for building low-power speech, acoustic event detection (AED), and sensor ML applications. The Raspberry Pi Pico is also a flexible microcontrollable board, programmable in C and MicroPython, which is adaptable to a variety of AI applications and skill levels. The RP2040 yet another microcontroller chip designed by Raspberry Pi, with two fast cores and plenty of on-chip memory, supports TensorFlow Lite models and is ideal for ML applications in general. The Raspberry Pi 4 model B and Raspberry Pi 400 are among other devices from Raspberry Pi which provide a complete desktop experience while offering fast networking, great energy efficiency, and low costs.

## 5.8 SUMMARY

In this chapter, we presented a conceptual framework to adopt EdgeAI in Algorithmic Government. We then talked about network integration and resource management which highlights the need for context-aware and self-governing network architectures to incorporate heterogeneous EI services. There is also the problem of resource allocation to ensure the seamless working of the entire network comprising of various edge devices, cloud servers, and fog nodes. We also discussed the difficulties faced to ensure an effortless collaboration of the edge and cloud to execute applications efficiently. We also elaborated on the need for edge devices to be reliable, self-sufficient, and resource efficient to be able to implement time-sensitive and critical use cases (such as AI in healthcare, industrial safety, border security) of algorithmic government. Followed by this we briefly discuss ethical issues which may arise while adopting EdgeAI, and few emerging solutions which aim at addressing these problems. In the end we provide an implications section which reinforces the purpose of the book by illustrating the need for EdgeAI in federal agencies, followed by hardware level implications.

## 5.9    Conclusion

We first introduced algorithmic government and the motivation and benefits of AI in government agencies. We then reviewed the role of Large-Scale Decision-Making in the algorithmic government and how AI technologies are fused into decision-making processes to make them easier and more effective. After raising the issues with cloud and fog computing, the need for edge was established. We demonstrated how edge performs better than the other two architectures through some use cases, addressing the commonly known issues of data privacy, network congestion, and latency. We then provided a comprehensive survey of Edge Intelligence efforts conducted so far in recent research papers, including an overview of the architectures, Key Performance Indicators, and enabling technologies. We then proposed different architectures and frameworks/technologies to increase the efficacy of AI model training and specific to use cases of federal agencies. Finally, we discussed some challenges in the design of edge computing devices. Future research is needed to address these aforementioned challenges and identify the overarching architectures, frameworks, and technologies that will lead to a seamless blend of cloud, fog, and edge computing to bring forth the vision of ubiquitous AI. This book will be helpful for Data Engineers, Data Scientists, Cloud Engineers, Public Policymakers, Administrators, and Academicians.

# References

Jayakodi, N. K., Doppa, J. R., & Pande, P. P. (2021, November). A general hardware and software co-design framework for energy-efficient Edge AI. In *2021 IEEE/ACM International Conference on Computer Aided Design (ICCAD)* (pp. 1–7). IEEE.

Rimal, B. P., Van, D. P., & Maier, M. (2017). Mobile edge computing empowered fiber-wireless access networks in the 5G era. *IEEE Communications Magazine, 55*(2), 192–200.

Smith, S. F., Barlow, G., Xie, X. F., & Rubinstein, Z. B. (2013). *Surtrac: Scalable urban traffic control.*

Suleiman, A., Zhang, Z., Carlone, L., Karaman, S., & Sze, V. (2019). Navion: A 2-mw fully integrated real-time visual-inertial odometry accelerator for autonomous navigation of nano drones. *IEEE Journal of Solid-State Circuits, 54*(4), 1106–1119.

Varghese, B., Wang, N., Barbhuiya, S., Kilpatrick, P., & Nikolopoulos, D. S. (2016, November). Challenges and opportunities in edge computing. In *2016 IEEE International Conference on Smart Cloud (SmartCloud)* (pp. 20–26). IEEE.

Wan, W., Kubendran, R., Schaefer, C., Eryilmaz, S. B., Zhang, W., Wu, D., Deiss, S., Raina, P., Qian, H., Gao, B., Joshi, S., Wu, H., Philip Wong, H.-S., & Cauwenberghs, G. (2021). *Edge AI without compromise: Efficient, versatile and accurate neurocomputing in resistive random-access memory.* arXiv preprint arXiv: https://arxiv.org/abs/2108.07879

Wang, T., Wang, C., Zhou, X., & Chen, H. (2019, August). An overview of FPGA based deep learning accelerators: Challenges and opportunities. In *2019 IEEE 21st International Conference on High Performance Computing and Communications; IEEE 17th International Conference on Smart City; IEEE 5th International Conference on Data Science and Systems (HPCC/SmartCity/DSS)* (pp. 1674–1681). IEEE.

William, E., Schatsky, D., & Viechnicki, P. (2017). *AI-augmented government using cognitive technologies to redesign public sector work.* Deloitte University Press.

Zou, Z., Jin, Y., Nevalainen, P., Huan, Y., Heikkonen, J., & Westerlund, T. (2019, March). Edge and fog computing enabled AI for IoT-an overview. In *2019 IEEE International Conference on Artificial Intelligence Circuits and Systems (AICAS)* (pp. 51–56). IEEE.

Zhou, Z., Chen, X., Li, E., Zeng, L., Luo, K., & Zhang, J. (2019). Edge intelligence: Paving the last mile of artificial intelligence with edge computing. *Proceedings of the IEEE, 107*(8), 1738–1762.

# WEB LINKS

https://coral.ai/

https://digital-strategy.ec.europa.eu/en/library/ethics-guidelines-trustwort
  hy-ai

https://ico.org.uk/media/about-the-ico/consultations/2617219/guidance-
  on-the-ai-auditing-framework-draft-for-consultation.pdf

https://mythic.ai/products/m1076-analog-matrix-processor/

https://openmv.io/products/openmv-cam-h7-r2

https://standards.ieee.org/content/dam/ieee-standards/standards/web/doc
  uments/other/ead_v2.pdf

https://www.blog.google/technology/ai/ai-principles/

https://www.cyient.com/prlisting/corporate/cyient-provides-drone-based-
  surveillance-technology-to-support-telangana-state-police-in-implementing-
  covid-19-lockdown

https://www.ibm.com/artificial-intelligence/ethics

https://www.intel.com/content/www/us/en/products/details/processors/
  movidius-vpu/movidius-myriad-x.html

https://www.microsoft.com/en-us/ai/responsible-ai?activetab=pivot1%3aprim
  aryr6

https://www.nvidia.com/en-in/data-center/edge-computing/

https://www.pdpc.gov.sg/Help-and-Resources/2020/01/Model-AI-Govern
  ance-Framework

https://www.raspberrypi.com/products/raspberry-pi-4-model-b/

https://www.syntiant.com/ndp100

# BIBLIOGRAPHY

Abiteboul, S., & Dowek, G. (2020). *The age of algorithms*. Cambridge University Press.

Aggarwal, M. (2017). Learning of aggregation models in multi criteria decision making. *Knowledge-Based Systems, 119*, 1–9.

AI Now (2018). *Litigating algorithms: Challenging government use of algorithmic decision systems*. AI Now Institute.

Ali, S., & Ghazal, M. (2017). Real-time heart attack mobile detection service (RHAMDS): An IoT use case for software defined networks. In *30th Canadian Conference on Electrical and Computer Engineering* (CCECE) (pp. 1–6).

AlMendah, O. M., & Alzahrani, S. M. (2021). Cloud and edge computing security challenges, demands, known threats, and vulnerabilities. *Academic Journal of Research and Scientific Publishing, 2*(21), ISSN: 2706-6495.

Avasalcai, C., Murturi, I., & Dustdar, S. (2020). Edge and fog: A survey, use cases, and future challenges. *Fog Computing: Theory and Practice*, 43–65. https://doi.org/10.1002/9781119551713.ch2

Badia, A. (2019). *The Information manifold: Why computers can't solve algorithmic bias and fake news*. MIT Press.

Baer, T. (2019). *Understand, manage, and prevent algorithmic bias: A guide for business users and data scientists*. Apress.

Baghban, H., Rezapour, A., Hsu, C. H., Nuannimnoi, S., & Huang, C. Y. (2022). Edge-AI: IoT request service provisioning in federated edge computing using actor-critic reinforcement learning. *IEEE Transactions on Engineering Management* (pp. 1–10).

© The Author(s), under exclusive license to Springer Nature Singapore Pte Ltd. 2023
R. Gupta et al., *EdgeAI for Algorithmic Government*,
https://doi.org/10.1007/978-981-19-9798-3

Batarseh, F. A., & Yang, R. (Eds.). (2017). *Federal data science: Transforming government and agricultural policy using artificial intelligence.* Academic Press.

Calo, S. B., Touna, M., Verma, D. C., & Cullen, A. (2017, December). Edge computing architecture for applying AI to IoT. In *2017 IEEE International Conference on Big Data (Big Data)* (pp. 3012–3016). IEEE.

Chang, L., Zhang, Z., Li, P., Xi, S., Guo, W., Shen, Y., Xiong, Z., Kang, J., Niyato, D., Qiao, X., & Wu, Y. (2022). *6G-enabled Edge AI for metaverse: Challenges, methods, and future research directions.* arXiv preprint arXiv: https://arxiv.org/abs/2204.06192

Christian, B., & Griffiths, T. (2016). *Algorithms to live by: The computer science of human decisions.* Macmillan.

Cummings, M. L. (2004). Automation bias in intelligent time critical decision support systems. *AIAA Intelligent Systems Technical Conference.* https://doi.org/10.2514/6.2004-6313

Kang, D., Emmons, J., Abuzaid, F., Bailis, P., & Zaharia, M. (2017). Noscope: Optimizing neural network queries over video at scale. *Proceedings of the VLDB Endowment, 10*(11), 1586–1597.

Dai, Y., Xu, D., Maharjan, S., Qiao, G., & Zhang, Y. (2019). Artificial intelligence empowered edge computing and caching for internet of vehicles. *IEEE Wireless Communications, 26*(3), 12–18.

Danaher, J., Hogan, M. J., Noone, C., Kennedy, R., Behan, A., De Paor, A., Felzmann, H., Haklay, M., Khoo, S.-M., Morison, J., Murphy, M. H., O'Brolchain, N., Schafer, B., & Shankar, K. (2017). Algorithmic governance: Developing a research agenda through the power of collective intelligence. *Big Data & Society, 4*(2), 2053951717726554.

Deng, S., Zhao, H., Fang, W., Yin, J., Dustdar, S., & Zomaya, A. Y. (2020). Edge intelligence: The confluence of edge computing and artificial intelligence. *IEEE Internet of Things Journal, 7*(8), 7457–7469.

Dietvorst, B. J., Simmons, J. P., & Massey, C. (2016). Overcoming algorithm aversion: People will use imperfect algorithms if they can (even slightly) modify them. *Management Science, 64*(3), 1155–1170.

Dillon, T., Wu, C., & Chang, E. (2010, April). Cloud computing: Issues and challenges. In *2010 24th IEEE International Conference on Advanced Information Networking and Applications* (pp. 27–33). IEEE.

Ding, R. X., Palomares, I., Wang, X., Yang, G. R., Liu, B., Dong, Y., Herrera-Viedma, E., & Herrera, F. (2020). Large-scale decision-making: Characterization, taxonomy, challenges and future directions from an Artificial Intelligence and applications perspective. *Information Fusion, 59*, 84–102.

Dressel, J., & Farid, H. (2018). The accuracy, fairness, and limits of predicting recidivism. *Science Advances, 4*, 1–5.

Ebers, M. (2021). *Algorithmic governance and governance of algorithms: Legal and ethical challenges.* Springer Nature.

Ebers, M., & Navas, S. (Eds.). (2020). *Algorithms and law.* Cambridge University Press.

Edwards, E., & Lees, F. P. (Eds.). (1974). *The human operator in process control.* Taylor and Francis.

Endsley, M. R. (2017). From here to autonomy: Lessons learned from human–automation research. *Human Factors, 59*(1), 5–27.

Engin, Z., & Treleaven, P. (2019). Algorithmic government: Automating public services and supporting civil servants in using data science technologies. *The Computer Journal, 62*(3), 448–460.

Engstrom, D. F., Ho, D. E., Sharkey, C. M., & Cuéllar, M. F. (2020). *Government by algorithm: Artificial intelligence in federal administrative agencies* (NYU School of Law, Public Law Research Paper, pp. 20–54).

Gamito, M. C., & Ebers, M. Algorithmic governance and governance of algorithms: An introduction. In *Algorithmic Governance and Governance of Algorithms* (pp. 1–22). Springer.

Gong, C., Lin, F., Gong, X., & Lu, Y. (2020). Intelligent cooperative edge computing in internet of things. *IEEE Internet of Things Journal, 7*(10), 9372–9382.

Guimaraes, R. G., Rosa, R. L., De Gaetano, D., Rodriguez, D. Z., & Bressan, G. (2017). Age groups classification in social network using deep learning. *IEEE Access, 5*, 10805–10816.

Gupta, R., & Pal, S. K. (2021). *Introduction to Algorithmic government.* Palgrave Macmillan.

Gupta, R., Muttoo, S. K., & Pal, S. K. (2017). *E-governance in emerging economy: Development et assessment.* Scholars World a division of Astral International Pvt. Limited.

Gupta, R., Muttoo, S. K., & Pal, S. K. (2017, March). Development of e-governance in an emerging economy like India: Assessment and way ahead for key components. In *Proceedings of the 10th International Conference on Theory and Practice of Electronic Governance* (pp. 613–616).

Hatvany, J., & Guedj, R. A. (1982). Man-machine interaction in computer-aided design systems. In *Proceedings IFAC/IFIP/IFORS/IEA conferernce analysis, design and evaluation of man-machine systems.* Pergamon Press.

Hosanagar, K. (2020). *A human's guide to machine intelligence: How algorithms are shaping our lives and how we can stay in control.* Penguin Books.

Javadzadeh, G., & Rahmani, A. M. (2020). Fog computing applications in smart cities: A systematic survey. *Wireless Networks, 26*(2), 1433–1457.

Johannsen, G. (1982, September). Man-machine systems: Introduction and background. In *Proceedings of IFAC/IFIP/IFORS/IEA conference on analysis, design and evaluation of man-machine systems, Baden-Baden.* Pergamon Press.

Kalpokas, I. (2019). *Algorithmic governance: Politics and law in the post-human era*. Springer Nature.

Kamruzzaman, M. M., Alrashdi, I., & Alqazzaz, A. (2022). New opportunities, challenges, and applications of Edge-AI for connected healthcare in internet of medical things for smart cities. *Journal of Healthcare Engineering, 2022,* 1–14.

Kearns, M., & Roth, A. (2019). *The ethical algorithm: The science of socially aware algorithm design*. Oxford University Press.

Leinberg, J., Lakkaraju, H., Leskovec, J., Ludwig, J., & Mullainathan, S. (2018). Human decisions and machine predictions. *Quarterly Journal of Economics, 2018,* 237–293.

Liu, B., Shen, Y., Chen, X., Sun, H., & Chen, Y. (2014). A complex multi-attribute large-group PLS decision-making method in the interval-valued intuitionistic fuzzy environment. *Applied Mathematical Modelling, 38*(17–18), 4512–4527.

Lovén, L., Leppänen, T., Peltonen, E., Partala, J., Harjula, E., Porambage, P., Ylianttila, M., & Riekki, J. (2019). *EdgeAI: A vision for distributed, edge-native artificial intelligence in future 6G networks*. The 1st 6G Wireless Summit (pp. 1–2).

Maclaurin, J., Liddicoat, J., Gavighan, C., Knott, A., & Zerilli, J. (2019). *Government use of artificial intelligence in New Zealand*. The New Zealand Law Foundation.

Margulies, F., & Zemanek, H. (1982). Man's role in man-machine systems. In *Proceedings IFAC/IFIP/IFORS/IEA conference analysis, design and evaluation of man-machine systems*. Pergamon Press.

McMahan, B., Moore, E., Ramage, D., Hampson, S., & Arcas, B. A. (2017, April). Communication-efficient learning of deep networks from decentralized data. In *Artificial intelligence and statistics* (pp. 1273–1282). PMLR.

Mukherjee, M., Matam, R., Shu, L., Maglaras, L., Ferrag, M. A., Choudhury, N., & Kumar, V. (2017). Security and privacy in fog computing: Challenges. *IEEE Access, 5,* 19293–19304.

Newell, A., & Simon, H. A. (1972). *Human problem solving*. Prentice Hall.

Osoba, O. A., & Welser IV, W. (2017). *An intelligence in our image: The risks of bias and errors in artificial intelligence*. Rand Corporation.

Pal, S. K. (2019). Changing technological trends for E-governance. In *E-governance in India* (pp. 79–105). Palgrave Macmillan.

Parasuraman, R., & Manzey, D. H. (2010). Complacency and bias in human use of automation: An attentional integration. *Human Factors, 52*(3), 381–410.

Peeters, R., & Schuilenburg, M. (2018). Machine justice: Governing security through the bureaucracy of algorithms. *Information Polity, 23*(3), 267–280.

Pohl, J. (2008). Cognitive elements of human decision making. In G. Phillips-Wren, N. Ichalkaranje, & L. C. Jain (Eds.), *Intelligent decision making: An AI-based approach* (pp. 41–76). Springer.

Ramasubramanian, A. K., Mathew, R., Preet, I., & Papakostas, N. (2022). Review and application of Edge AI solutions for mobile collaborative robotic platforms. *Procedia CIRP, 107*, 1083–1088.

Rimal, B. P., Van, D. P., & Maier, M. (2017). Mobile edge computing empowered fiber-wireless access networks in the 5G era. *IEEE Communications Magazine, 55*(2), 192–200.

Schnoll, H. J. (2015). *E-government: Information, technology, and transformation*. Routledge.

Schultze, U., Aanestad, M., Mähring, M., Østerlund, C., & Riemer, K. (Eds.). (2018). *Living with monsters? Social implications of algorithmic phenomena, hybrid agency, and the performativity of technology: IFIP WG 8.2 Working Conference on the Interaction of Information Systems and the Organization, IS&O 2018, San Francisco, CA, USA, December 11–12, 2018, Proceedings* (Vol. 543). Springer.

Shi, W., Cao, J., Zhang, Q., Li, Y., & Xu, L. (2016). Edge computing: Vision and challenges. *IEEE Internet of Things Journal, 3*(5), 637–646.

Shi, Y., Yang, K., Jiang, T., Zhang, J., & Letaief, K. B. (2020). Communication-efficient Edge AI: Algorithms and systems. *IEEE Communications Surveys & Tutorials, 22*(4), 2167–2191.

Slack, J. D., & Hristova, S. (2020). Why we need the concept of algorithmic culture. In *Algorithmic culture: How big data and artificial intelligence are transforming everyday life* (p. 15). Lexington Books.

Surden, H. (2014). Machine learning and law. *Washington Law Review, 89*, 87.

Tang, M., & Liao, H. (2021). From conventional group decision making to large-scale group decision making: What are the challenges and how to meet them in big data era? A state-of-the-art survey. *Omega, 100*, 102141.

Tolan, S. (2018). *Fair and unbiased algorithmic decision making: Current state and future challenges* (JRC Digital Economy Working Paper 2018-10). European Commission.

United States. Executive Office of the President. (2016). *Artificial intelligence, automation, and the economy.*

Xu, D., Li, T., Li, Y., Su, X., Tarkoma, S., Jiang, T., Crowcroft, J., & Hui, P. (2020). *Edge intelligence: Architectures, challenges, and applications.* arXiv preprint arXiv: https://arxiv.org/abs/2003.12172

Yang, L., Lu, Y., Cao, J., Huang, J., & Zhang, M. (2021). E-tree learning: A novel decentralized model learning framework for Edge AI. *IEEE Internet of Things Journal, 8*, 11290–11304.

Ye, Y., Li, S., Liu, F., Tang, Y., & Hu, W. (2020). EdgeFed: Optimized federated learning based on edge computing. *IEEE Access, 8*, 209191–209198.

Yeung, K., & Lodge, M. (Eds.). (2019). *Algorithmic regulation*. Oxford University Press.

Zafar, M. B. (2019). *Discrimination in algorithmic decision making: From principles to measures and mechanisms*.

Zhou, Z., Chen, X., Li, E., Zeng, L., Luo, K., & Zhang, J. (2019). Edge intelligence: Paving the last mile of artificial intelligence with edge computing. *Proceedings of the IEEE, 107*(8), 1738–1762.

Zuiderveen Borgesius, F. (2018). *Discrimination, artificial intelligence, and algorithmic decision-making*.

# INDEX

© The Author(s), under exclusive license to Springer Nature Singapore Pte Ltd. 2023
R. Gupta et al., *EdgeAI for Algorithmic Government*,
https://doi.org/10.1007/978-981-19-9798-3